# DO YOU KNOW
# WHO I AM?

BOOK PUBLISHING INFORMATION
traitmarkerbooks.com
traitmarker@gmail.com

ATTRIBUTIONS
Editor: Robbie Grayson III
Cover Design: Robbie Grayson III

PUBLICATION DATA
Paperback: 9781088120156

Interior Title & Text Font: Minion Pro
Interior Text Font: Minion Pro
Interior Title Fonts: Minion Pro

Printed in the United States of America.

# DO YOU KNOW
# WHO I AM?

*An Infantryman's Adoption Story*
*of Finding Family after Fifty*

## CHRISTOPHER E. HARVEY

TRAITMARKER BOOKS

# 988

## SUICIDE &
## CRISIS LINE

# DEDICATION

*We dedicate this book to the more than 3.5 million Iraq, Afghanistan, Gulf War, Vietnam Veterans, and their families for whom the Honoring Our Promise to Address Comprehensive Toxins (PACT Act) of 2022 will cover the medical care and benefits that they deserve. To the surviving spouses, children, and family members: may all the advocacy and actions of so many involved in this historical law bring you peace.*

## CHRIS HARVEY | RENO, NEVADA
### *FEBRUARY 2023*

# SEQUENCE OF EVENTS

DISCLAIMER (x)

DEDICATION (xi)

PROLOGUE
*On the Origin of My Species* (xiii)

CHAPTER 1 | Unnatural Selection
*Birth Through Kindergarten* (18)

Original Sin | *Birth*
A Private Exchange | *Meeting My Adoptive Parents*
Passing Through the Waters | *Baptism*
"The Year of Turmoil and Change" | *1968*
Loss #1 | *The Three-Wheeler Accident*
Sibling #1 | *The Birth of My Oldest Sister*
TIPS FOR ADOPTEES #1

CHAPTER 2 | Wonderful Life
*Kindergarten Through Second Grade* (32)

Historical Event #1 | *Apollo 17*
Kindergarten | *(1972-1973)*
Sibling # 2 | *The Birth of My Only Brother*
Historical Event #2 | *The Oil Crisis*
Exodus | *Moving to California*
Loss #2 | *JimmyJohn*
TIPS FOR ADOPTEES #2

CHAPTER 3 | River Out of Eden
*California* (40)

Promised Land | *Life in Southern California*
Historical Event #3 | *Operation Frequent Wind*
The Big Scare | *"You're Dad Had a Heart Attack"*
TIPS FOR ADOPTEES #3

CHAPTER 4 | The Immense Journey
*Fourth Through Eighth Grade* (49)

Wandering in the Wilderness | *Coming Back
  to Northern Nevada*
Dad's Open Heart Surgery | *(1978)*
Sibling # 3 | *The Birth of My Middle Sister*
The Big Tell | *"You're Adopted"*
Historical Event #5 | *The Iranian Hostage Crisis*
Historical Event #6 | *Operation Eagle Claw*
Dad's Stroke | *(1980)*
Historical Event #7 | *Reagan Assassination Attempt*
TIPS FOR ADOPTEES #4

CHAPTER 5 | The Descent of Man
*High School* (69)

Looking for Someone to Call Home | *Freshman Year
  Through Fall of My Junior Year*
Running Away | *(1984)*
Switching High Schools | *(1984)*
Sibling #4 | *The Birth of My Youngest Sister*
Finishing High School | *(1985)*
TIPS FOR ADOPTEES #5

CHAPTER 6 | The Selfish Gene
*Right after High School* (79)

Starting University | *(1985)*
Starting Community College | *(1986)*
Historical Event # 8 | *The Challenger Disaster*
TIPS FOR ADOPTEES #6

CHAPTER 7 | The Making of the Fittest
*United States Army* (84)

First Marriage | *(1986)*
Basic Training | *(1986)*
Hawai'i Deployment & the 25th Infantry
   Division Light | *(1986-1988)*
The Divorce | *"I'm Not Coming Back"*
Loss #3 | *Dad's Death*
TIPS FOR ADOPTEES #7

CHAPTER 8 | The Third Chimpanzee
*Army Reserve, Reserve Deputy Sheriff
& Correctional Officer* (99)

Second Marriage | *(1988)*
Army Reserve | *(1988-1992)*
Community College: Second Time Around | *(1988)*
Reserve Deputy Sheriff & Correctional Officer | (1988-
   1990)
The Foreign Affair | *"It's Over"*
Community College | *Third Time Around (1990)*
Third Marriage | *(1990)*
Historical Event #9 | *The Gulf War*
Offspring #1 | *The Birth of My Oldest Daughter*
TIPS FOR ADOPTEES #8

### CHAPTER 9 | On Human Nature
*Blood Is Thicker Than Water* (109)

University | *Second Time Around*
Community College | Fourth Time Around
(1991-1996)
Offspring #2 | *The Birth of the First Person I Ever Knew
    Who Was Related to Me*
Final Marriage
TIPS FOR ADOPTEES #9

### CHAPTER 10 | The Mismeasure of Man
*Life in My 30's* (114)

Finally, a Degree | *(1997)*
Offspring #3 | *The Birth of My Son*
Historical Event #10 | *9/11*
Community College | *Fifth Time Around (2005)*
My Coronary Artery Bypass Surgery | *(2005)*
University | *Third Time Around (2006-2008)*
Getting My Associate of Applied Anthropology |
    (2006)
TIPS FOR ADOPTEES #10

### CHAPTER 11 | The Blind Watchmaker
*Life in My 40's* (124)

Receiving My Bachelor's Degree | *(2008)*
Starting a Master's Degree | *(2008)*
Loss #4 | *Father's Death*
Working for the Boy Scouts of America | *(2011-2014)*
My Daughter's Pup | *(2011)*
Exiting My Master's Degree | *(2011)*

Historical Event #11 | *Air Race Disaster*
Loss #5 | *Mom's Death*
Wildfire | *(2011)*
Loss #6 | *Brother's Death*
Moving to a New University | *(2014)*
Getting My MBA | *(2015)*
Going to Culinary School | *(2015-2016)*
Tips for Adoptees #11

## Chapter 12 | The Greatest Show on Earth
### *All Hell Breaks Loose* (136)

Starting My Doctorate | *(2016)*
The Ancestry.com Message | *"Do You Know Who I Am?"*
The Call | *"I Want to Meet You"*
The Meeting | *"This Is My Daughter"*
The Confession | *"I'm Sorry I Lied"*
  *Search Squad*
  *My Search Angel*
  *Permission to Search*
  *The Search*
  *Search Concluded*
The Letter | *"I'm Your Son"*
The Call | *"I'm Your Mother"*
The Meeting | *"Well, I Suppose That You Are My Mother"*
Family Reunion | *(2018)*
The Trip | *"So, You Are My Brother?"*
Loss #7 | *The Pup Dies*
Tips for Adoptees #12

## Chapter 13 | The Ancestor's Tale
### *Relationships* (156)

My Birth Mother | *Blood*
My Oldest Sister | *Babysitter*
My Middle Sister | *Blondie*
My Youngest Sister | *Baby*
My Maternal Grandmother | *Bitch*
Tips for Adoptees #13

## Chapter 14 | Darwin's Dangerous Idea
### *What Lies Ahead* (169)

Life Will Find a Way
Grief & Loss
The Cousin Acquaintance
Old Battle Buddies
Isolation
Tips for Adoptees #14

## Epilogue
### *Now You Know The Rest of the Story* (180)

The Final Frontier | *"And That's the Way it Is"*

## Acknowledgments (184)

*Photo Gallery*

*About the Author & Contact*

# Disclaimer

This work depicts actual events in the life of the author as truthfully as recollection permits. While all persons within are actual individuals and while the author has chosen not to use actual names and some identifying characteristics of family members, no characters have been invented and no events have been fabricated.

The conversations in this book all come from the author's recollections, though they are not written to represent word-for-word transcripts. Rather, the author has retold them in a way that evokes the feeling and meaning of what was said and in all instances, the essence of the dialogue is accurate.

# DEDICATION

*To my parents, both adoptive and birth, nurture and nature—*

I wouldn't be the person I am today without the contributions of each of these four people. Two gave me what I needed, most of what I wanted, and taught me to be full of curiosity. Two gave me life, and no matter how that turned out, I am grateful.

*To my wife—*

Thank you for supporting me in more ways than one. I am not the easiest person to live with, but you are always there. You put up with more than anyone should, but I do my best to care for you and I believe that is what gets you through. Thank you for being a second mother to my daughters and the mother of our son. I know that isn't an easy job.

*To my children—*

You are all the joy of my life. I do my best to be there for each of you and take care of what I can. I also do my best to let each of you live your lives. I am proud of each of you, more than you know. I have an endless supply of love for each of you.

*To my uncle—*

The Infantry says "Follow Me" and follow you I did. Your time led you to Korea and Vietnam, while mine led me to a very Cold War. I followed you as best I could, but all I could do is what I was asked. The Army puts their soldiers where they want them, and I did my duty.

*To my sisters, all three of them—*

You all have certainly made life interesting. What our future holds, I have no idea.

*To the rest of my family, both adoptive and birth—*

I love you all. Hopefully, we all will meet someday, and it would be my honor.

*To the men and women of the Armed Forces and our First Responders—*

You are my brothers and sisters. While I love my Infantry brothers, every servicemember is important. All I ask is for everyone to be proud of the role they played.

*Family comes in many shapes and forms!*

# PROLOGUE
## On the Origin of My Species

As I sit here on Christmas Day 2021, I am beginning this memoir with the hope that it will help other adoptees like me. In August 2018 at the age of 51, I connected with my birth mother and youngest sibling for the first time. While some of my questions were answered, others began. I will save that for later in the book.

Approximately 5 million adoptees live in the United States. With the current U.S. population at 336 million, that means 1½% of Americans are adopted. That statistic alone puts adoptees in a unique demographic. And while it goes without saying that all human beings are unique in their own ways because they each possess a specific ancestral lineage, their own personal life experiences, and occupy a specific space in time, the strangeness I felt when meeting blood relatives for the first time and the mysterious circumstances surrounding my adoption have made me feel especially alien, even among other adoptees. So this is a story about my differences.

I served as an Infantryman in the United States Army. Half of 1% of the U.S. population is currently serving in the armed forces, and only 6% percent have ever served. I also have bachelor's and master's degrees. Of the population over 25 years old, 27% have a bachelor's degree and 13% have a master's degree. I'm sure you might know someone who has served in the Army—even someone who is a Veteran Infantryman. You also might know someone in the Army who has both bachelor's and master's degrees. But who do you know is both and adopted? It isn't impossible, but statistics say that the percentages are low.

As you will come to know, my childhood ended in 1979 when I was twelve years old. That was the year that my adoptive mom (rather vindictively) disclosed to me that I was adopted. Looking back, I believe that singular event has affected my ability to trust people.

My story deals with the three themes of trust, understanding, and love intertwined with the facts that I am adopted, its impact on the unfolding of my life, and the isolation that I feel daily because of it. Most of the people whom I trust are also the people I love. Few there are whom I trust and love.

Insofar as understanding, it is a difficult concept for me to grasp. While I wish to understand those around me, I still find it difficult. Why? Probably because I haven't had their experiences. On the other hand, the same goes for those I know. They also have difficulty understanding me because they haven't walked 25 miles in my shoes (Infantrymen will understand the reference to 25 miles).

Woven throughout my story are a few historical American events that have shaped our culture and world events as well as my own life. If I didn't believe that America was a great country, I never would have served in the Army. The historical information I include that happened before I was old enough to remember is based strictly on historical accounts that I have read as a student of history. The ones that come after I was old enough to remember are based on my own recollections and are chosen based on their impact on my life at the time.

Because this is the story of my life and because I value the chronology of historic events, I'm laying out my story in chronological order, even some events that occurred in my birth family before meeting them at age 51. While telling a story this way might undermine a lot of the mystery that usually accompanies such writing, one of my purposes is to create a template that could be useful to any reader who is looking for answers to their own origins.

## A NOTE ON TERMS

When I use the term *parent* or *parents,* I am speaking about my adoptive parents. Additionally, I refer to my adoptive parents in the singular with the affectionate *mom* and *dad.* I refer to my birth parents with the formal terms *mother* and *father.* As far as siblings, I was the only child of my [adoptive] parents. So, the only siblings I have are from my [birth] mother and father. Therefore, all my siblings are full siblings. My Godparents are my Godparents by proxy unless otherwise noted. They stood in for my real Godparents who were my aunt and uncle on my adopted dad's side of the family.

## A NOTE ON "FRIENDS"

I don't have friends. If you believe that you are a friend of mine, don't take offense. It is simply easier to define people as friends with whom I currently spend time or have had a long affectionate relationship. However (and with few exceptions), anyone mentioned as a friend is what most people would refer to as an acquaintance.

Relationships with military people are different. Naturally, there is a fundamental level of trust. Most of those relationships, however, are long in my past, and I do not have many military friends now.

## TIPS FOR ADOPTEES

At the end of each chapter I will include tips for adoptees who are thinking about or in the process of looking for their birth families. These tips are not exhaustive and are mainly based on my own life situation and search.

As an adoptee, the best thing you can do is *what you feel is right.* It's my hope that some of these tips will help you.

I would like to thank everyone who reads this book.

Not only do I hope that it helps you to understand my life but that—like a mirror—it might make some sense of your own. I wish you the best life. One that you can't even imagine.

CHRIS HARVEY | RENO, NEVADA

Not only do I hope that it helps you to understand
my life but that—like—it might make some
sense of your own ... the best life. One that
you can't even imagine.

CHIEF HART, RENO, NEVADA

## CHAPTER 1
# Unnatural Selection
### Birth Through Kindergarten

*I hate that her headstone has a year on it for when
she was born and another for when she died but
only a dash for the life she lived in between.*

JULIANN GAREY

ORIGINAL SIN (BIRTH)

My life began at 10:02 a.m. on Saturday, April 22,
1967. Like all the newly born, I had no opinion at the
time on how life would transpire for me. My mother
was all but 15 on the day I was born. Far too young
to bring me to full term by today's standards. My father wasn't much older: just a young man of 16. While
some might call their mishap "irresponsible" and others "unfortunate,", I later learned that neither of them
wanted to give me up for adoption.

But those hopes weren't to be. My maternal grandparents insisted that my mother give me up. To ensure

that, she was forced to sign papers relinquishing custody of me. So far as my father's involvement, I imagine that he had no choice in the matter. After all, he was underage as well, was not married to my mother, and grew up during a time when such a consideration likely didn't include his opinion.

What is clear is that their firstborn child was taken from them, and they had no choice in the matter. After doing my due diligence by interviewing witnesses and conducting what amateur sleuthing I learned along the way, I can confirm that my mother's and father's hearts were broken at the decision. This pivotal point of their pubescent years would affect both of them for the rest of their lives. But from the time my mom leaked the dirty little secret of my adoption until I learned to my satisfaction that I was wanted, my own heart would be broken for those intermittent years, not knowing why I was given away.

I eventually found my birth family much later, though not all of them. But for the meantime, my mother only got to see me once before I was taken away and I do not believe that my father ever laid eyes on me. As a parent myself, I can't imagine what a parent in that situation would feel, and I can't imagine how every waking moment would not be preoccupied with what became of their little one.

## A PRIVATE EXCHANGE
## (MEETING MY ADOPTIVE PARENTS)

My parents picked me up on April 25, 1967, from one of the local hospitals where my mother had given birth to me. At three days old, I was introduced to my parents that I would believe for the next 12 years of my life were my natural parents. *Natural,* of course, refers to biological or birth parents. I still have pictures of that day, including one of me in the back seat of a car without a car seat. Those were the days when "safety" and "liability" weren't things that people thought about like they do today.

I know that my adoptive parents were happy to have me in their lives. You can tell by their facial expressions in the pictures, and I can testify to this truth in the myriad ways they treated me while growing up in their house. There isn't much more I can say about the day we met, but it is a day, I later learned, that changed the lives of a countless number of people.

One set of parents left the hospital happy while another set left distraught.

## PASSING THROUGH THE WATERS (BAPTISM)

My dad was born in New Orleans, Louisiana. Of French ancestry, he was raised Roman Catholic and lived through the Great Depression. While he was a devout Catholic, his marriage to my mom happened outside the church because she was not a member of the faith nor would she convert until I was a young teenager. Having said that, she did not stop him from practicing his faith and attending church regularly. So, when it came for their adopted son to "pass through the waters," I was to be baptized and raised Catholic. Members of my dad's family who were chosen to be my Godparents would not travel to attend my baptism. As a result, my parent's best friends stood in as Godparents by proxy.

I was baptized in one of the local Catholic churches on Sunday, April 30, 1967. From what I know, Catholic baptisms on Sundays were and still are common. What might not be common (even in those days) was for the baptism to be announced in the local newspaper. Well, at least the way mine was. The announcement was less of an announcement and more of an article—hell, even an advertisement—recognizing my parents, highlighting my dad's occupation, mentioning the names of my Godparents and their proxies, and a large photo of the baptism as proof.

I often wondered if my mother and father had seen this in the newspaper. That thought by itself has led me to come up with a number of scenarios of how that might have happened. I always assumed that they gave me up because they didn't want me. So, seeing me in the newspaper wouldn't have mattered in that scenario. Based on what I know now, I can't help but think that my father and mother might have been able to put some of the pieces together of why the connection between my young mother, father, and me had to be kept a secret: why the deception had to be so complete at all costs. Pieces that we all have now. Pieces that blow the mind.

## "THE YEAR OF TURMOIL AND CHANGE" (1968)

Many historians have described 1968 as a pivotal year in American history. Though an amateur historian at best, I have sat through several lectures on "The Cultural Decade" in which the specific year 1968 played a central role. In my own research and experience, I can affirm that it was an incredible year in which many signature events rocked the foundations of our great country.

While technically I fall within the age range of Gen X (born 1965-1980), I don't entirely align with their experiences. I was raised by a dad who was a World War II Veteran and a mom who was a homemaker. Because both were older than average parents and because I disliked school, my relationship with my parents was tighter than normal, and I was raised probably like most Boomers were (born 1946-1964). But then that's not entirely true either.

Around the time that I started walking, talking, developing my personality, and formulating my first impressions and memories of the world around me, it was 1968. It's fair to say that I was "coming of age" during a year in which cultures clashed in such a way that ensured that the United States of America would never be the same. Six of these events oddly influenced my upbringing.

## TET OFFENSIVE

The Tet Offensive was one of the largest military operations of the Vietnam War. Beginning on January 30, 1968, the Viet Cong (VC) and North Vietnamese People's Army of Vietnam (PAVN) launched an offensive against the South Vietnamese Army of the Republic of Vietnam (ARVN), the United States Armed Forces, and their allies. The impact of this offensive was something I have thought about often while growing up. At the time these events began, I wasn't even a year old. However, the Tet would last well into the Fall of 1968 while its consequences echo down to this very day with the loss of thousands of lives, including American lives. General Westmoreland shocked the nation when he disclosed that the Vietnam War effort would require 200,000 American men as well as activation of the reserves. Was there not one community somewhere in our great nation that was not disrupted by this announcement?

My mom was close to her younger brother and never missed one week talking to him at least once a week for most of his life. My uncle was a Combat Infantry Veteran of the Korean War and he was in Vietnam during 1968, serving in the U.S. Army. Between the wars, he served with the Los Angeles Fire Department as a fireman. Second to the powerful influence of my dad, my uncle was the most influential role model in my life. His role as an Infantryman in the Army undoubtedly influenced my own. I had great respect for both men. I still do.

## MURDER OF MARTIN LUTHER KING, JR.

Civil Rights Leader Martin Luther King, Jr., was assassinated on April 4, 1968, in Memphis, Tennessee. Many believe that James Earl Ray was just a scapegoat and that the assassination was a governmental conspiracy. Ironically, Martin Luther King's nonviolent platform found him speaking against the Vietnam War a few weeks before he was murdered. While so much controversy around his death is still debated today, the sum total effect was that Luther's death proved to be devastating to our nation. The fight for Civil Rights and Equality remains at the forefront of our nation.

I believe that everyone deserves to live their best lives. That can't happen until everyone has the same fundamental rights, are equal in the eyes of the law, and have fair access to the opportunities that come their way: life, liberty, and the pursuit of happiness. Many of the problems of the world can be solved if each of us championed these fundamental God-given rights for others as we do for ourselves.

It isn't that easy, I understand. But for someone who has felt an outsider for the majority of his life, I get the dream of Martin Luther King, Jr. It has been my own.

## MURDER OF ROBERT F. KENNEDY

Presidential Candidate and Senator Robert F. Kennedy was assassinated on June 5, 1967, in Los Angeles, California. Many believed that he was our nation's next great hope, just as his brother John F. Kennedy had been earlier considered. Kennedy was assassinated by Sirhan Sirhan who shot him through a hotel kitchen window of the Ambassador Hotel when Kennedy was taking a short cut to the press room. We can only guess the course of the nation had his brother not been assassinated in 1963 while serving as President of the United States, but the same is true of Robert F. Kennedy. He was a huge proponent of progress from the Civil Rights Movement to disrupting organized crime to finding a solution to the Vietnam War.

Being baptized a Roman Catholic, I take it to heart that John F. Kennedy was the first Catholic President of the United States and that his presidency happened in the tumult that was the 1960s. A significant number of Americans at the time were against having a Catholic president. While it's true that our country was based on the ideal that church and state be separate, it stings somewhat to acknowledge that a President of the United States was so discriminated against for his personal religion. I'm sure that all of our presidents have had a religious affiliation each has privately favored over others.

Another thing that hits close to home is the kind of coordination of minds and efforts within the Kennedy family. Clearly, they had great plans for our country and had a large number of supporters. What strikes me as both beautiful and sad, however, is how much good that such closeness and unity of purpose among those with blood ties could have on the greater good.

## OLYMPIC BLACK POWER SALUTE

On October 16, 1968, two Black American athletes raised their hands in protest at the Summer Olympics in Mexico City, Mexico. Olympian runners Tommie Smith and John Carlos during the American National Anthem raised their closed fists in what was soon to become the widely recognized symbol of Black Power. If you have no context for the kind of impact their gesture had, consider Colin Kaepernick taking a knee in protest during the American National Anthem. Anyone who was familiar with the National Football League, the San Francisco 49ers, or our country's continued civil unrest should be familiar with his protest.

It seems that the more we push to realize our democratic ideals in our nation, the more things fundamentally remain the same. My old boss was famous for saying, "If we keep doing the same things, we're going to get the same results." He also said, "Hope is not a strategy." Both are classic quotes. Both quotes leave a lot to be desired in the way our country moves towards its democratic ideals in which all people are given a fair chance at life, liberty, and the pursuit of happiness. As an adopted child who for the most part of my life has felt as if I didn't belong, I understand the pain behind the raised fist. I also understand that waiting around for other people to make your life easier doesn't always (or ever) work. The best advice I can give is, "Be the change you want to see in the world."

## FIRST INTERRACIAL KISS ON AMERICAN TELEVISION

On November 22, 1968, the science fiction television series *Star Trek* (Season 3, episode 10) broadcasted the first interracial kiss on national television. Captain James T. Kirk (William Shatner) kissed his communications officer, Lieutenant Nyota Uhura (Nichelle Nichols) who was Black. For what many considered a mediocre series at the time, this was groundbreaking television at its finest and (whether or not it was intended) in support of the Civil Rights freedoms that was splitting the country down the middle.

One of the premises of *Star Trek* is that the traditional divisions of race, gender, and nationality are a thing of the past. Pushing it further, *Star Trek: The Next Generation* introduced a society where people only worked for the good of the community, which was the community of the planet. What a utopia that Gene Roddenberry created for us and what balls he had to do it when he did.

I can speak on behalf of a fair number of adoptees. When separated from your blood kin and you feel like you don't belong, the definition of family gets broadened out of pure necessity. While I have a biological mother and father, my mom and dad are those who raised me as their son.

## APOLLO 8 & APOLLO 11

I have always been fascinated by space flight. Not only was my dad an avid reader of science fiction (he had been a fan of Buck Rogers), but *Star Trek* was the first TV show that I remember watching as a kid. As a child, I understood that *Star Trek* was pure television fiction. But when I learned later that Apollo 8 actually orbited the moon, something shifted within me.

Three astronauts, Frank F. Borman, II, James A. Lovell, Jr., and William A. Anders, crewed the mission that launched on December 21, 1968, and splashed down in the North Pacific on December 27, 1968. As a nation, we were one step closer to putting a man on the moon and bringing him safely back to earth which would happen by the end of the decade. And that happened on July 20, 1969 (a promise, by the way, made by the late President John F. Kennedy).

The Apollo lander Eagle landed on the moon on July 20, 1969. One astronaut, Michael Collins, remained in the command module (CM) while Buzz Aldrin and Neil Armstrong landed on the moon. Armstrong would be the first person to step onto the moon. All three of them returned to the Earth on July 24, 1969. As Tom Hanks stated in *From the Earth to the Moon*, "When will we be going back, and who will that be?"

When I was able to appreciate these events later on

as a young child, I was impressed with the notion that *dreams do come true.* What you imagine *can,* if you allow it, come to pass. With the civil unrest of the 1960's coming to a head and the launch of space exploration, I can't help but wonder how my exposure to those events figured into my own aspiration to find a family that, like an alien race, had done a great job hiding from me my entire life. And all of this before I was out of diapers.

## Loss #1 (The Three-Wheeler Accident)

One of my earliest personal memories is what I call "The Three-wheeler Accident." As it goes with one's earliest memories, I don't remember exactly when it happened, but I know that it was when we were living in the first house my parents owned after my adoption.

I had a three-wheeled toy that I spent a lot of time on. It wasn't exactly a tricycle and it was made of plastic. One early morning when I was out riding before my dad went to work, I had been riding it and left it in the driveway. When my dad left and I was watching him back out of the garage, he promptly backed over it and destroyed it.

Of course, he didn't do it on purpose. He couldn't see it from the front seat. Before that point, I couldn't recall having ever seen anything as distressing as the destruction of beloved possession, especially by someone I loved. The suddenness, violence, and confusion of it all made me so upset that I could not stop crying. I remember my dad comforting me and telling me not to worry. He would get me a new one. *But what about this one?*

He never said it was my fault, but I was smart enough to know that it was. I was also smart enough to know that if he couldn't buy another one, I had no one to blame but myself.

I think that's what most of the crying was: knowing that it was my fault for leaving the toy where it shouldn't have been. I'm sure that my dad bought me another one but I don't remember that (and I wonder why I don't). I do know that my parents took care of all my needs and many of my wants. I was a lucky little guy with very loving parents. The only problem was that I would later discover that they were not my natural parents.

## SIBLING #1 (THE BIRTH OF MY OLDEST SISTER)

To keep with the chronology of events, something else I didn't know during this time in my life was that my biological parents had another child. I should back up.

Sometime between 1967 and 1971, my biological mother and father married. I could look up the date myself or ask my mother, but that isn't important to me right now. What was important many years later was that my oldest younger sibling, a sister, was born in July 1971. I would have been four years old.

**TIPS FOR ADOPTEES**
*WHEN DID YOU FIND OUT OR DISCOVER
THAT YOU WERE ADOPTED?*

- *Late Discovery Adoptees (LDA's) are usually defined as individuals who discover they were adopted only after they become adults.*

- *Most individuals who find out they are adopted as a child usually learn before they start school (i.e., under six years old).*

- *Some statistics say that about 3% of children find out they were adopted after they are six years old.*

- *If you are an LDA, you should take time to sort out your feelings before you make any other decisions. If you need help, reach out for help.*

- *If you find out you are adopted in your childhood after the age of six, it would be helpful if your adoptive parents help you with the feelings you experience.*

- *At some point in your life, you will choose whether or not you want to search for your birth family. That decision is yours.*

- *If you do decide to search for your birth family, you should never give up. You might find your family, you might find that they have passed, or you might never find them. Of course, there are many other possibilities.*

## Chapter 2

# Wonderful Life

### Kindergarten Through Second Grade

*Space is for everybody. It's not just for a few people in science or math, or for a select group of astronauts. That's our new frontier out there, and it's everybody's business to know about space.*

CHRISTA MCAULIFFE

### Historical Event #1 (Apollo 17)

There are a couple of significant things at this point that I remember. I remember watching *Star Trek* and watching *M\*A\*S\*H*. Late in 1972 three more astronauts made the voyage to the moon. I would bet that a lot fewer people know their names than those who know the names of the astronauts who were on Apollo 11.

The mission was similar to that of Apollo 11 with Ronald E. Evans remaining in the command module (CM) while Eugene A. Cernan and Harrison Schmitt landed on the moon in the lunar module (LM) *Challenger.* To this day, Cernan and Schmitt are the *last* two men to walk on the moon.

What made this mission so spectacular to me was that I watched it on television. Now I can't recall how much coverage there was (and there might not have been much), but it seemed to me that the entire mission was televised. I do know that my dad made sure that I saw whatever was broadcasted. I remember looking up at the moon and saying to myself, *Wow, there are men up there right now.* My fascination and awe are probably due to the fact that I am part of a generation that was alive before man walked on the moon.

## KINDERGARTEN (1972-1973)

I never spent a day in daycare, with a nanny, or in preschool. On the few occasions that my parents did have to attend a social gathering, I would have a babysitter. My mom was a stay-at-home parent which was common in their circle.

My dad, on the other hand, was a self-made man who owned his own construction company. In fact, he was one of the last individuals in the state to have an unlimited contractor's license.

In the Fall of 1972, I started kindergarten at the public school for which I was zoned. Before I began kindergarten, I used to spend some of the day with my dad on a construction site and then the rest of the day with my mom until my dad returned home for dinner.

We usually had dinner on the floor in the den, sitting in front of the television watching a show like *Star Trek*, *M\*A\*S\*H*, or whatever happened to be on. In the early 1970s, most people had access only to three networks, and no one had VCRs or DVRs. There was no MTV or child-oriented shows around dinner time, so you watched what was on if you watched television at all.

Once I started kindergarten, I would attend school in the mornings. On some days my mom would pick me up and we would go home. On other days my dad would get me and we would go to a construction site. Not much changed to my schedule except the interruption of a few hours of school in the morning.

School was boring to me. All I remember doing in kindergarten was ABCs and 123s, watching movies played on a projector and screen, the teacher reading to us, learning to read, and taking naps. I already knew my ABCs and 123s and could read a little, so most of the activities we did were redundant and an interruption in my original schedule which I found more engaging and exciting. The only thing I looked forward to at school was getting picked up and taken home or to my dad's construction site.

One other thing that I remember about school was that there was a street right across from the school that was named after our last name because my father built the first house on that street. There was also a neighborhood right around the corner from the school with a couple of streets named after my dad's construction company. Not far from where I currently live, there is a 77-home subdivision that was built by my dad in 1966.

The streets inside the subdivision were named after people who helped my dad get that project off the ground. Throughout the region, there are probably around 200 homes that my dad built. Every once in a while when I happen to drive by one of these houses or streets, it brings back all kinds of memories. Most of them are good, but they always cause me to miss my dad. A few of the houses have been torn down with new houses built in their place. This seems like sacrilege to me, but life goes on for the living. Change is inevitable.

## SIBLING # 2 (THE BIRTH OF MY ONLY BROTHER)

My biological mother and father had another child born in March 1973. This time, I had a little brother, and he was the 3rd (III), named after my father who was Junior (II), and my grandfather who was Senior (I). I learned that my mother and father had named me before I was born, knowing full well that they were not going to be able to keep me. I haven't asked, but maybe that is why I wasn't the 3rd (III).

My brother was born prematurely, and he suffered lifelong problems because of congenital problems. I would love to have known my brother. He and my father both sound a lot like me, and it would have been nice to know members of my family who were like me.

My mother and sisters are dissimilar from me in a number of ways, that I know. However, with my brother and father both passing before I found my birth family, I have no way to compare our similarities. There isn't a day that I don't think of both and wonder how life could have been different had I known them.

## HISTORICAL EVENT #2 (THE OIL CRISIS)

I started first grade at one of the local parochial (Catholic) schools in the Fall of 1973. The school offered first through eighth grades. My grade was a class of about twenty that year. Even though it was a private school and probably cost my parents some good money, I found school to be boring there, too. In fact, I didn't pay much attention to what was going on most of the time.

I was not an A student (I believe they did give letter grades then in the lower grades), and I seem to imagine that there was a play that year in which I played Old King Cole.

The most impressionable memory I have during first grade was the Oil Crisis. It was on television all the time. I remember seeing cars lined up for what might have been blocks (or what even seemed like miles to me) in other cities. Where I lived, the lines were usually a block or two long. In comparison to what I saw on television, it didn't seem like we had to wait too long in line.

The oil crisis began because America was supposedly running out of oil. I remember that gas was under a dollar a gallon before the crisis started and that it jumped to over a dollar for the first time during that period. That was a major problem for the gas stations as you might imagine. You could think of it as Y2K (2000). Everyone was worried about the computer rolling over to the year 2000 during Y2K (computers were programmed to roll back to 1900). Similarly, gas pumps weren't set up to go past $0.99 at the time because they were analog and not digital like most of the world today. This was a big deal and disruptive to say the least.

## Exodus (Moving to California)

When school started in the Fall of 1974, I was all set for another year of boredom. Sometime earlier in the Summer or Spring of that year, my Godparents sold their business (a local hotel), packed up their small farm, and moved to Southern California. Their main interest in their farm had been raising thoroughbred horses. They tried to convince my parents to move with them. When my parents and I visited later, I don't think my parents were too impressed. However, one of my dad's doctors told him that it might be better for his health to move to a lower elevation. Southern California had lower elevations, so my parents considered moving. When my dad was younger, he had surgery to clear out a blockage in either his abdominal or infrarenal aorta. For whatever reasons, the doctors highly recommended the move. As best I recall, we packed up and moved right after school had started. They settled in a city north of San Diego.

## Loss #2 (Jimmy John)

It was around this time that I recall another traumatic experience that changed me. My parents had our house on the market, and there had been a few people who came to see it. We had a Dachshund (wiener dog) at the time.

Once when we were showing the house, our dog was with us. The next thing I knew, I saw a rather large dog run through our yard and attack our dog. It grabbed him by the throat and wouldn't let go. As young as I was, I immediately started to run toward the dogs. My dad grabbed me to prevent me from getting in the middle of it. I protested and told him that I was going to save our dog.

The people who were touring our house began to call out to the other dog. That was when we realized the dog belonged to them. When their dog finally released our dog, we all knew it was bad. My mom told the people to leave, and my dad immediately rushed our dog to the veterinarian. He returned home after a while, but the injuries were too severe and our dog had to be put to sleep.

The three-wheeler incident was a lesson in the loss of a possession I considered irreparable. However, I learned the day that my dog was attacked what it was like to love something so much that I was willing to give my life for it. Sitting here now, I am crying tears of sorrow. This is one of the few times that a living thing will be named in this book. Our little wiener dog was named Jimmy John, and I will never forget him or the love that I had for him.

TIPS FOR ADOPTEES
*THREE WAYS TO LOCATE YOUR BIRTH FAMILY*

- *Ask your adoptive parents or other adoptive family members if they have any information about your birth parents or family.*

- *Obtain your Original Birth Certificate (OBC) or sign up for the national or state registry in states that have closed adoption. Also, get your nonidentifying information if possible.*

- *Take a DNA test. The preferred testing sites are Ancestry, 23andMe, and MyHeritage. Ancestry has the largest database of tested individuals, so it is likeliest that you would find a match there. That is not a guarantee that you will find a match directly with your parents or potential siblings. It's just the most comprehensive option of the three I've mentioned.*

# CHAPTER 3
# River Out of Eden

## CALIFORNIA

*This is to be mortal,
And seek the things beyond mortality.*

### LORD BYRON

### PROMISED LAND (LIFE IN SOUTHERN CALIFORNIA)

I don't know how we got everything in our house from Northern Nevada to Southern California. We might have paid movers, but I don't remember. What I do remember is that my Godparents drove their pickup truck to Northern Nevada and loaded it up with some of our possessions. My dad loaded up his truck, and my mom loaded up her car as well. There was also a U-Haul, trailer, or something similar. My godfather drove the U-Haul back down and the rest of us followed.

I am pretty sure that I rode with my dad all the way. We had a nice stop for lunch in Bishop, California, which was a waystation for us on many trips back and forth from Northern Nevada to Southern California. Plus, we had a spot we would always stop to eat hard-boiled eggs that we brought with us and a particular gas station where we stopped called "Four Corners." I still make that trip today. The restaurant in Bishop isn't the same, and sometimes we do fast food there. Sometimes we don't take hard-boiled eggs. But we almost always stop at "Four corners."

When we settled into our new house, it was the second one that I had ever lived in that my dad did not build. The first house I lived in was not one he had built. There wasn't time to build a house before moving because we moved quickly. My dad bought two lots about a block away from this house and started building our new home as well as a spec house almost immediately.

I have a lot of memories of the house he built for us. I also have a lot of memories of the home that my Godparents built for themselves. They had purchased a small ranch when they moved but built their own house. Even though my godfather wasn't a contractor, he did his best. I still have a picture of my parents and me in my Godparents' new house. Our new house was right on the golf course just as a couple of others had been in Northern Nevada. I have lived on a golf course ever since.

One of my first memories of living in Southern California was experiencing an earthquake. It wasn't a major quake, but it wasn't small either. I don't know its magnitude, but it rocked us for almost a minute. I have lived through some other smaller quakes and one or two that might have been close to the same size as that first one. Some were in Southern California and some were in Northern Nevada. There was a year here in Northern Nevada when we had a series of quakes. While I'm not afraid of quakes here in Northern Nevada, I hear that California might have a big one anytime. And that won't be pretty.

My parents wanted to keep me in a parochial school but the only one in the town that we lived in was not accepting new students. They couldn't get me into any in the area that year. I skipped most of the second grade because of that, only having attended for about a month in Northern Nevada before we moved. They found a school that would take me the following year, but it was a thirty-mile drive each way twice a day. They did enroll me there for the following year. Once I went there, I wasn't too thrilled about spending two hours on the road each day to go to school, but what's a kid to do? In the meantime, my parents asked the principal if they could recommend a private tutor for me so that I wouldn't fall behind. There was a young lady, right out of college, who had been hired to teach third grade the next year and she was looking to make some money. She was whom the school suggested. My parents hired her after meeting her for an interview.

I hope my parents got their money's worth out of my tutor. We didn't spend too much time on schoolwork, but she would pick me up several times a week to go on an adventure. We hit the beaches north of San Diego as far up as Oceanside. We'd go to parks, and I'd do a little schoolwork and then play a lot. We went to the San Diego Zoo and the Wild Animal Park north of San Diego. I wouldn't call her a tutor or a babysitter, she was more like a fun older sister. Her name was Suzie and when the year was over, and it was time for third grade to start she was my teacher. That was the only year I attended school there. I already knew my teacher but no one else at the school knew her since she was just starting. I haven't had contact with her since then, but it would be fun to find her and at least talk and laugh about all the fun we had.

I made a close friend when I attended school in Southern California with whom I would meet up again in high school. This kid was the only person who I befriended when we lived down there. I have thought about him many times since moving back to Northern Nevada. It would be great to see him again. At least I think it would be. The way that we met in high school was built on a lie. That isn't the way that I wanted it to be, but that's how it happened at the time.

My family and I spent a lot of weekends at my Godparents' house. My mom's parents lived just a couple of hours away, and we would visit them occasionally or they would come to see us. It was the same with my aunt and uncle (the one who was a Korea and Vietnam Veteran). I also got to know my cousin a little during that time.

We had a lot of fun down there, and we spent a lot of

time in the swimming pool at our home or with my Godparents. I spent a few nights at my Godparents' house the Summer between what would have been my second- and third-grade years. My Godmother had one of her nieces (or grandnieces) living with her for three of four weeks during the Summer. She was from Texas where my Godmother was born. I loved her Southern accent, and we had fun swimming together, and having adventures around the farm. Looking back, that was the first time that I felt that I liked a girl. She was pretty and looked nice in her swimsuit. Granted, we were both eight years old. I am sure that I had a little crush on her. However, I never saw her again after that Summer and couldn't tell you her name even if I wanted to.

## HISTORICAL EVENT #3 (OPERATION FREQUENT WIND)

My uncle seemed to be acting a little differently in the Spring of 1975. I can't point to anything specifically as to why that was, but I think it was because he knew the war in Vietnam either was going to escalate or come to an end pretty quickly. Operation Frequent Wind proved to be the beginning of the end of the Vietnam War.

I am not too clear on the history of the events during this time, but I know that a week after I turned 8, an extensive airlift effort to evacuate people from different locations in Saigon took place. The evacuation lasted two days from April 29-30, 1975. What

I remember clearly is that all remaining Americans and some Vietnamese nationals evacuated Saigon. I remember watching the news and seeing helicopters airlifting people from the roof of the U.S. Embassy. Either then or shortly after that, I knew the war was over. I knew that soldiers had died during the war, but I didn't know why. But what I did know within the next seven or eight years was that I wanted to be a soldier.

My dad served in the Navy during WWII as a corpsman. He didn't stay in for long after he finished training because he had a medical condition of which the Navy was unaware and they discharged him. He had been unaware of his condition as well. All he wanted to do was serve. It was unfortunate that his condition was a disqualifier.

My dad eventually got over not being able to serve, unlike many others in his position at the time. It wasn't unheard of for a young man to kill himself after finding out that he was "4-F". Many young people felt the call of duty during WWII. I felt that calling myself when my time came, just for different reasons. My mom's stepfather and older brother were both on the beaches of Northern France on D-Day. My mother's other brother was in Korea and Vietnam as I mentioned earlier. These are some of the reasons that I felt the call: legacy. It was a family tradition to serve, and I took that seriously as I grew into a young man.

## THE BIG SCARE ("YOU'RE DAD HAD A HEART ATTACK")

After being in Southern California for about a year, my parents returned to northern Nevada for a week to visit friends and for my dad to play in a golf tournament. I stayed with my mom's parents. My step-grandfather (whom I didn't know was my step-grandfather for many years) took me to do a number of fun things which included getting McDonald's quite a few times, taking me to 7-Eleven for Slurpees and comic books, and other various activities I enjoyed at that age. We might have even played a round of golf ourselves.

I also remember him introducing me to Carl's Jr. That was the first time I had a burger with anything other than cheese, mayonnaise, mustard, and ketchup. Even though I had a burger with the works there, I didn't like it very much. Maybe that was because everything squirted out of the bun and all over me. I do still enjoy Carl's Jr. on occasion, just with fewer toppings.

It was on the third or fourth day when I was staying with my grandparents that my grandma got a call in the middle of the day. That wasn't all that usual, but I heard her whispering to someone. She made a call right after that and did some more whispering. My grandpa wasn't there at the time. He was a partner in a private security company and had to go into the office to solve a problem (even though he was supposed to be off while I was staying with them).

He said that he needed to stay in the office until

5:00 p.m. but that he would be home shortly after. He showed up at the house about 20 or 30 minutes after my grandmother's phone calls. At that point, I knew something was up. He sat me down while my grandma went to make some snacks and told me he had some news to tell me. He said that wasn't sure what to tell me or how I would react.

I asked him if it was about my parents, and he said that it was about my dad. He then told me that my dad had not been feeling well during his golf game and thought that he might have had heartburn. After my dad finished his round, he went to see one of his doctor friends in his office. When his friend came into the waiting room to say hello, he immediately knew that something was wrong when he saw my dad.

They quickly went into another doctor's office in the building, a cardiologist. That doctor said that it was apparent my dad was having a heart attack, so they rushed him to the hospital across the street in a wheelchair. Of course, my grandpa didn't tell me all of this then. He just said, "Your dad has had a heart attack." I ended up learning all these details a few weeks later when my parents returned to Southern California.

My dad was lucky to have survived. At the time my grandpa told me, I had never been more afraid in my life. I was so afraid that my dad would die that I am pretty sure I had what now would be called a panic attack. I was shaking and had no clue what to do. Thankfully, my panic passed and my dad recovered. However, this wasn't the end of his health problems.

He spent some time in the hospital over the next year in Southern California. I recall that there was a time that he was hospitalized for five to seven days. He did not like the care that he received in Southern California which was in a Kaiser Hospital just north of San Diego. He didn't like that there was a new doctor every day and that they didn't know anything about him or his case. I think this might have been a decisive factor in our moving back to Northern Nevada.

The Summer after third grade, my parents again went back to Northern Nevada to visit friends and play in a golf tournament. I believe this cemented their desire to move back to the area, and it wasn't long until we were there. I started the fourth grade after the move and right on time with everyone with whom I had gone to school before we moved.

### TIPS FOR ADOPTEES
#### CONSIDER YOUR REASONS FOR SEARCHING FOR YOUR BIRTH FAMILY

- *Do you want to know your family and medical history?*

- *Do you want to know why you have certain physical traits such as eye and hair color?*

- *Are you looking for closure?*

48

# Chapter 4
# The Immense Journey

## Fourth Through Eighth Grade

*A terminal illness forces us to make every
second count, whereas the forces of boredom
make us count every second.*

### Mokokoma Mokhonoana

## Wandering in the Wilderness
## (Coming Back to Northern Nevada)

About a year after my dad's heart attack, my parents
decided that we would move back to Northern Nevada before the start of the new school year. The move
happened just like the move to Southern California
but in reverse. It was in 1976 and my Godparents and
other relatives in Southern California were disappointed. I think it was as nice for them with us living
there as it had been for my mom and me. After all, we
got along well with her family and my Godparents:
they enjoyed the time spent with their godson, grand-

son, nephew, and cousin as well. The same was true of my mom with her friends, brother, nephew, mom, and stepfather.

Like I said, my dad wasn't happy with the healthcare system in Southern California. He didn't have a permanent cardiologist because the system was set up to see whoever was available. Because he liked the cardiologist in Northern Nevada, my mom agreed to move.

Life in Northern Nevada resumed after the move in what I can only describe as normal: I was bored in school. The area had changed noticeably when we returned. That is to say, it was growing. We started shopping at the same grocery store as when we lived there before. Some of the employees recognized my dad because he was a memorable guy. Part of that memorability was that he was one of only two customers of that store who had a personal charge account. The other individual was the owner of one of the local casinos.

My dad had worked for the casino owner when he and my mom first moved to Northern Nevada and they had become friends. The casino was also the sponsor of the golf tournaments that my dad had been returning to play in when they vacationed those two years while we lived in Southern California. The store manager was shocked to see my dad. He had thought that my dad had passed away when he abruptly stopped shopping there. Maybe my dad should have closed his line of credit before we left, and the manager would have known differently!

## DAD'S OPEN HEART SURGERY (1978)

It wasn't long after returning to Northern Nevada that my dad had another heart attack. It wasn't as bad as the first one, but the cardiologist decided to run more tests to try to determine the extent of the damage. I remember my dad having a heart catheterization procedure, one in which they shoot dye into the circulatory system to watch the heart. It was determined that he had various levels of blockage in several arteries. They suggested that he schedule an appointment with a heart surgeon at Stanford.

Open heart surgery wasn't as common then as it is today. One of the surgeons at Stanford was Dr. Norman Shumway who performed the first adult heart transplant in 1968. His partner was Dr. Edward Stinson who was the chief resident who assisted with the transplant. My dad met these two doctors, and they reviewed everything. I believe that they performed their own catheterization procedure.

After several days of meetings and additional testing, they advised that he have open-heart surgery. They said that the number of bypasses would be determined by the viability of the veins harvested from his legs during the first part of the two-part surgery. He scheduled his surgery with the surgeons and returned a month or so later for the procedure.

I remember the surgery starting the day before Thanksgiving in 1978. They estimated that the surgery would last well over twenty-four hours. There was a special waiting room where my mom and I waited alone. We had been there for a couple of days already with my dad being in the hospital for pre-op tests. Things didn't move as quickly back then compared to now.

We were told that a scrub nurse would come out to give us updates every couple of hours. That happened for the first twenty-four hours or so. There came a point when it had been three or four hours since we had received an update, and my mom and I became nervous and anxious. Finally, Dr. Stinson came out (if my memory is clear). He told us that the surgery had been difficult and taken longer than they expected, but that the arteries in my dad's legs had allowed them to perform a triple bypass. It was late Thanksgiving night when the surgery was complete.

At one point while we were waiting in the waiting room, a nurse delivered us Thanksgiving dinner with turkey and all the trimmings. She said that a doctor's wife had dropped it off for us. The doctors' wives knew that their husbands were doing important work. In fact, I believe that several of the doctors' wives made dinner for the whole surgical team as well. We were told that they ate and took breaks in shifts while performing the surgery.

We didn't get to see my dad until the next morning. We had been at the hospital for over 48 hours at that point. We spent some time with him that morning and then the doctors insisted that we return to our hotel to get some rest. If we didn't, they admonished, we wouldn't be useful in helping my dad.

The hotel wasn't too far away, and I remember it was decorated in a Hawaiian motif with lots of tikis and tiki torches: I found it strange. My dad had to remain in the hospital for three weeks of observation. The nurses brought us lots of meals while we were there. We also ate in the cafeteria a few times and went to a restaurant once or twice.

When it was close to the time that my dad was going to be released, the doctors met with my mom to discuss transportation home and follow-up care with his cardiologist. They wanted my dad to get home quickly. This left out the four-plus-hour drive. They also didn't want him to fly. It was the old Catch-22. In the end they allowed him to fly if a responsible person flew with him. At 11 I couldn't drive, so that meant that my mom had to get the car home. We thought of having my Godmother or a Southern California relative fly in to fly home with my dad. But for whatever reason, we couldn't get someone there at the right time.

With a little bit of convincing the doctors agreed that I could accompany my dad on the airplane. My mom left the day before so that she could be there to pick us up. The hospital sent my dad and me in an ambulance, and we were treated like VIPs at the airport and on the airplane. The doctor's office had arranged everything. This wasn't something that had happened too many times in the past. My dad did fine on the airplane, and the trip was uneventful. I was proud that I was able to help him out.

Sometime during this process, the doctors told my dad that he could expect to live another four to six years. It hit me then that I would not have my dad in my life for much longer. I grew up a lot during this time, and I prayed every night that God would let my dad have a few more years, more than the four to six that the doctors estimated. Without the surgery, my dad probably would have died within the year, so anything more than that was a gift. But I wanted more. Who wouldn't?

I constantly made deals with God, and I told him that he could shorten my life if he would only let my dad live more than six years. At the time my greatest hope was that my dad would live to see me graduate high school and that there would be time for me to learn enough about the construction business to take over his business. I wanted it to provide for his legacy and to carry on his name so that no one would ever forget him.

At the same time I knew I wanted to serve my country. I had no idea how I would do both, but it would be something I would have to figure out in the near future. College wasn't something that I knew about at this time, and it wasn't something that my parents talked about ever.

## SIBLING #3 (THE BIRTH OF MY MIDDLE SISTER)

Near the end of the 1978-1979 Winter, my natural parents would have another child who would be my third full sibling: their second daughter. I was almost 12 years old when this happened. The older siblings were born when I was four years old and the next when I was close to turning six, respectively. If I had not been adopted, my middle sister seems to be the sibling whom I might have understood better than the other two.

What I mean by that is that it probably would be harder to understand what having a sibling meant at a younger age. At 12 I would have a better grasp of the situation. After meeting all my siblings later, it was this sister who made me understand more about sibling relationships than the others. That has nothing to do with loving each of them less or more. It's only that I spent more time together with this sibling than the others. The relationship felt closer and stronger because we had more time to get to know each other.

## The Big Tell ("You're Adopted")

Shortly after I turned 12 in the Spring of 1979, I experienced the most confusion in my short life. However, it also proved to be a time when some things became clearer.

One evening before dinner, my mom came into my room. She told me that dad was home and that dinner would be served soon. Then she also said that she had something to tell me. She hesitated, almost as if baiting me. I fell for it. *I* asked her what it was.

She then said (as casually as if she were telling me

that it was time for dinner) that she just wanted to tell me that I was adopted.

"Excuse me? What did you say? Did you just say what I think you said?"

Her response was something to the effect of, "I've said what I have to say." Then she walked out of the room.

I sat there for a few minutes, thinking about what I had just heard. A little while later, she called down the hall that dinner was ready, and I went out to eat. No one said anything during dinner. I stewed on this new revelation for a couple of days, probably until that Saturday. When I was getting ready to get into my dad's car that morning to go somewhere with him that I now forget, I addressed the situation.

"What is this about me being adopted?"

Surprised and somewhat disappointed, he told me that if I needed answers then I needed to talk to my mom. Talk about passing the buck.

I waited a few days. One night before dinner, I asked my mom to tell me more about my being adopted. Imagine my surprise when she told me that she had no idea what I was talking about! It was a long time before I would broach this subject again. From that point on I never mentioned it again to my dad. When he had told me to talk to my mom, I remember the sadness in his words. I saw it in his eyes. I read it in his body language.

I think that moment was when I cognitively understood that I could read people and read them well. It is a skill I have used many times in my life, and it is almost 100% accurate.

I only ever brought up the subject of my adoption to my mom a handful of times after that day. Her response was always the same: denial. I know that I told her a couple of times that I hated her because she wasn't my birth mother. She went to her deathbed and never again admitted that she wasn't my birth mother.

It wasn't until I returned home after my time in the Army that I realized my mom had mental issues. The term for what she did a lot of the time while I was growing up wasn't common back then: gaslighting. She would always tell me things in the affirmative and then either deny them or tell me one thing and then say another. There were times in my life when I thought that I was mentally unstable or that I was going to lose my mind because of her antics.

My mom was good at convincing me that what I knew had happened had *never* happened. It wasn't until I married my current wife that I got a handle on this. She would play the same games with my wife. Once we began to compare notes, we realized without a doubt that this was a systemic problem with her. It was easier to confirm this behavior when there was a witness to it other than myself. Like my wife.

Thank God that we quickly came to understand that we weren't crazy. She was simply trying to manipulate us. But she never did this to anyone else. That isn't to say that she didn't manipulate others, but gaslighting wasn't her method with them. The rest of the world thought she was an angel, and everyone she met loved her. A family member later told me after she had passed that they were pretty sure she was bipolar. And that other members of her family were, too.

There were many times that my mom's behavior made my wife and I look like fools to other people. We couldn't ever prove that she was gaslighting us because she was tactical. She would make sure that we were unprepared for her new "disclosure". We always wanted to catch her on tape, with a video recorder, or with audio or video on our phones, but we never could. One reason is that we didn't want her to know we were trying to do it. Because if she caught us, she would have just said that she was joking. I'm sure that even if we had been successful, it wouldn't have mattered. She had a way of manipulating anyone and everyone to believe whatever she wanted.

My dad was one of the smartest people I have ever known. He was pretty much a savant. I can't believe that he didn't know what was going on. However, he did pass away before I had put all the pieces together and before this behavior became out of control. I know that he loved her with every fiber of his being, I have never known anyone who loved someone as much as I believe that he loved her. His love for me was the same. Maybe he was blinded by love.

Other than this, what had become clear to me quickly after her revelation that I was adopted was the fact that I hadn't figured it out. Maybe I was blinded by love as well? No matter what my mom did or who she was, I believe that she loved me in much the way my dad loved each of us. But then it became clear to me that I was adopted.

I had previously picked up on the times that I wondered why I didn't look like my parents (or anyone else in the family for that matter). What threw me was that there was a kid or two in my school who didn't look like their parents either. So, I assumed that most kids looked like their parents, but some also didn't. I was just one of those who didn't.

My best friend from this young period in my life lost his brother last year. We ended up talking for the first time in many years because of this. Over the years his brother had become a close friend. I went over to my old friend's house because he had some things of mine that his brother held for me in his safe for safekeeping. When I picked up the things, we talked about finding my birth family and about my being adopted.

My old friend said he was surprised that I hadn't figured out that I was adopted before I was told. According to him, all the other kids in our class had assumed I was, including him. Not only that, but they had all talked behind my back about it and might have even made fun of me for not knowing.

All of this was shocking to me, but it explains why I never felt that comfortable around others and why I have very few friends. I don't trust people. Trust is earned and few people have earned it from me. I trusted most of my Army buddies with my life because they knew they could trust me with theirs. That was a brotherhood. I trust my wife with everything and my kids with most things. But that's it.

There are plenty of people whom I would have liked to trust. Maybe they seemed nice at first glance, but I would get the vibe that I couldn't trust them. I let people in up to a certain point, but every interaction is a test. Fail the test and you are untrustworthy. But the problem is that *sooner or later, everyone fails.*

I'm sure that this response is a product of not knowing for many years why my natural parents gave me up. They weren't trustworthy because they couldn't care for their child. But when I found out that this wasn't the case, I was relieved! But building that distrust like a muscle for decades, it's hard to relax it. My faith in people hasn't changed and that lack of trust in my birth parents for all those years is hard to undo.

I'm sure that it is also a product of never trusting my mom after her telling me that I was adopted and then never admitting it again. It is also a product of failed marriages. And most of all, it is a product of testing people and having them always fail.

My dad was trustworthy. He lived by a strict moral code, always doing what he said he would do. If he shook someone's hand and made a promise, it was as good as gold, as good as a legally binding contract, and he never once failed to come through. I live my life that way.

The military taught me a similar code. Anyone who cannot live up to that standard is untrustworthy and could never be more than an acquaintance. Even my old friend and his brother with whom I became friends didn't live up to the code. But I granted them an exception because life with no friends is lonely.

Living in a world full of people in a city that is neither large or small, I have always felt isolated because of my lack of ability to form friendships. I know that this will never change. I have my moral code, the code that my dad taught me, and the code that I learned in the military. I do what I say, and you can take that to the bank. If you can't do the same, we will never be friends. Even when I am with my wife and kids, I feel isolated. It isn't because they aren't there for me or I for them, but because I think people need more than just a small circle of trust or a couple of friends who are half in and half out because of an exemption.

The lack of family growing up added to this problem. The only time family was around on a semi-regular basis was when we lived in Southern California. Life was better during those years than ever before and forever since. Therefore, I had hoped that if I did search for and find my birth family, I could find some new family that I could trust. I trust a couple of family members in my birth family like I trust my kids: with some things. There will be more on this later when I discuss meeting my birth family and our relationships.

## HISTORICAL EVENT #5 (THE IRANIAN HOSTAGE CRISIS)

On November 4, 1979, there were 52 employees of the U.S. Embassy in Tehran, Iran, who were taken hostage. This was big news for our country and the world, and it was given news coverage every night. As the crisis went on, the television news would keep the public updated on the current day, such as "Day 99 of the Hostage Crisis in Iran".

By this time, I was beginning to figure out that we lived in a crazy world where people just couldn't seem to get along. I saw interviews of hostages' family members and saw how distraught they were and how much they wanted their family members back. I rooted for these hostages, hoping that they wouldn't be harmed and that they would be released soon.

I knew that the President and the government were working on this crisis. The President at the time was Jimmy Carter. For whatever reason (and believe me, I don't know) this was yet another moment in time when I knew that I wanted to serve my country. Maybe it was to make sure that these kinds of things never happened to my fellow countrymen.

## HISTORICAL EVENT #6 (OPERATION EAGLE CLAW)

Operation Eagle Claw was an attempt by Delta Forces on April 24, 1980, to rescue the hostages: just two days after I became a teenager and on my parents' anniversary. I can't remember if anyone knew about it beforehand, but my knowledge now tells me that it is highly unlikely that anyone did because of operational security.

The failed attempt was announced shortly after the mission failure occurred. I remember seeing a photo of a helicopter that had crashed along with hearing information about casualties. With me just six years away from joining the Army, I was gaining a greater understanding of how dangerous serving in the military was.

I knew people died in Vietnam, but my uncle had made it home. If he made it home, how dangerous could it be? None of this deterred my wanting to join the military.

## DAD'S STROKE (1980)

It was sometime around the Summer of 1980 that my dad had a stroke. He had been up in the attic, putting some things away or looking for blueprints of homes he had built in the past. The attic had blown insulation, so going up there wasn't fun, especially in the heat of the Summer. Between the heat and insulation, it was often hard to breathe up there for an extended period.

When my father came down, he was having difficulty breathing and his eyes were red and watery. That wasn't too unusual, but I could tell that there was something else wrong. I had been waiting at the bottom of the ladder for him to come down, and it only took me a matter of seconds to realize he was having a stroke.

After getting him seated and telling him that I was getting him some help, I told my mom that he was having a stroke and that we should call an ambulance. She didn't believe me.

"How would you know?" I told her that I just knew.

When she came into the garage, she still didn't believe it. Instead of calling the ambulance, she called a friend's son who was home for a short while over the Summer on a short break from medical school (or possibly as an intern). She described dad's symptoms and I yelled at her about other symptoms that I saw. Luckily, the person on the other line suggested calling an ambulance because it *did* sound like a stroke, and time was of the essence.

I believe that he wound up being in the hospital for a week or two. When he came home, he had more medication on top of that for his heart and was supposed to eat healthier. This was less than two years after his bypass surgery. I thought for sure that he was going to die, but he recovered. It wasn't more than a few months later, though, that he had another stroke.

After the second stroke, the doctors ran tests, had him see a neurologist, and worked together to come up with a solution. The solution was that they would scrape out the arteries in his neck on both sides. I am less familiar with these procedures than I am with open-heart surgery, so I can't provide more details.

A surgeon, possibly a neurologist, performed the

surgery. Before the surgery, they told us that if everything went well, he could come home in a few days to
a week. After surgery and recovery, he was moved to
a ward. He seemed to be conscious in recovery. However, he did not regain consciousness within the expected time, so he was moved to a semi-private room
and monitored. We were told that the surgery put too
much stress on him and that he was in a coma. They
hoped that he would come out of it in a few days. But
after a few days had lapsed, they said that he might
never come out of it. My mom would spend the whole
day with him. I had returned to school for the Fall
right before the surgery.

After school each day, I either would go to work a
four-hour shift if I had work or go straight to the hospital if I were off. On days I worked my mom would
pick me up after work and we would stay until about
9:00 p.m. We also would stay until 9:00 p.m. on the
nights I didn't work. This exhausted both of us.

This went on for a little over three weeks. One afternoon when we went straight to the hospital after
school, the nurse saw us and told us that dad had
come out of a coma while my mom had gone to pick
me up. They had asked him questions about his name,
where he was, and things like that to assess his mental
state. The nurse was discussing this with my mom but
asked that I go down the hall until they were done.
But it didn't matter. I could hear the discussion.

They had asked my dad to recollect something from
his past, and he had told the doctors of the time that

he and my mom had moved to Cuba about six to nine months before Batista was overthrown and Castro took over. At the time my dad worked in illegal gambling halls throughout the south and he went to work in the casinos in Cuba. The nurse told my mom that she and the doctors knew he had some serious mental deficits because his story was just that: a story that wasn't believable or even possible. But my mom told the nurse that she must be crazy, too, because she was there with him when they moved to Cuba.

The doctors were given this new information the next time they completed their rounds, and they made a release plan for my dad. He came home about a week later, and we had all survived another major medical emergency that could have been the end for him.

Things got back to the new normal quickly. I was back to getting more rest. At age 13 I had a part-time job and had held it for almost a year (I started when I was 12). I was the head of my department before I turned 13.

My mom was getting more rest as well, and my dad was taking it easy. My mom didn't have to worry about getting me to work or bringing me home afterward. At the time, we had a Vespa Moped and it wasn't illegal for me to operate it—license or not—so I could take care of myself. I excelled at that job, learned many management skills, and added to the knowledge that I had gained for the last six years, helping on construction sites, ordering lumber, writing my dad's checks, and keeping his books. Not normal things for a kid my age. My greatest hope was the same as after my dad's open-heart surgery: that he would live to see me graduate high school.

HISTORICAL EVENT #7
(REAGAN ASSASSINATION ATTEMPT)

President Reagan took office in January 1981, and the hostages were released shortly after that, making him the hero for securing their release (even though a lot of the leg work had been done by President Carter.). But just a little over two months after his inauguration, an attempt was made on the President's life on March 30, 1981.

When this happened, my school principal brought a television into our classroom for us to watch the story unfold. He said that we were watching history. Indeed, everything that we have experienced becomes history and a part of our history. But this, as it was happening, was one of those events that would make the history books for decades to come if not for centuries.

President Reagan was the first president who I learned a lot about. All I remember about President Carter was the Iranian Hostage Crisis and the fact that people made fun of him for being a peanut farmer (as well as the antics of his brother and Billy Beer). I would watch the news whenever President Reagan was mentioned or appeared.

Before President Reagan left office, not only would he be the Commander-in-chief of the U.S. Armed

Forces, but he would be *my* Commander-in-chief. And I can't express my excitement when I received a surprise award at a division formation, presented by one of Reagan's Undersecretaries of the Army. I would have gone through Dante's Seven Circles of Hell for my Commander-in-chief.

## TIPS FOR ADOPTEES
### CONSIDER ALL POSSIBLE OUTCOMES

- *You cannot find any information.*

- *They have passed away. This does not preclude finding possible full or half siblings or other family members.*

- *They have no desire to meet.*

- *One or both of your birth parents has a checkered past. Other family members could fall into this category as well.*

- *It's a happy reunion. Be thankful if that is what you were looking for.*

- *It is a not-so-happy reunion. This is a distinct possibility.*

- *You have some mixture of the above outcomes. Remember that there are other biological relatives besides your parents.*

# Chapter 5
# The Descent of Man
## High School

*Trust is like a mirror, you can fix it if it's broken,
but you can still see the crack in that
mother fucker's reflection.*

LADY GAGA

## Looking for Someone to Call Home
## (Freshman Year Through Fall of My
## Junior Year)

My high school years were the start of an interesting time in my life. As I mentioned earlier, I discovered that I liked girls while living in Southern California at the prepubescent age of 8. There were a few girls who I noticed between then and the time that I finished eighth grade. In high school, however, I started looking for a girl with whom to have a relationship. There were five of them throughout high school including one who shared my birthday. The relationship that I

69

had with two of them was more serious than the others. I still have contact with both from time to time, but one not as often as the other.

I knew that I needed to find someone with whom I could share my life: someone I could trust and someone that would love me. While my family loved me, I missed the love that could come from my biological relatives. That left a hole in my life, and I needed someone to fill it. Probably earlier than normal.

Freshman year was boring. School seemed hard, but there were a couple of classes I enjoyed, I had some new acquaintances, and there were a couple of teachers whom I liked. There were a few girls that I had some interest in, but not enough to act upon. There was the usual hazing, mostly with seniors and varsity football players who bullied people and pulled pranks on freshmen. I was bigger than almost anyone in the school at 6' 2" and about 180 lbs. I had thought that would keep me safe, but it didn't. What did keep me safe was the fact that when people tried to haze and bully me, I wouldn't take it. I'd give back better than they were giving. After a short while, no one was bothering me anymore. My freshman year was uneventful for that reason.

On the first day of my sophomore year, I saw a new girl coming down the steps from the second story of the school outside. I knew she was "the one". She was beautiful. For me it was love at first sight. I didn't act on my feelings for a month or so. I watched her when I would see her and tried to figure out who her friends were. I finally gathered the nerve to talk to her but struck out.

Later in the year, I tried to approach her again. I must have convinced her to give me a shot because we started hanging out together at school. But we weren't dating. This continued throughout the remainder of the year, and we did end up dating over the Summer. Then we broke up.

I met another girl after breaking up. The new girl and I started dating. We were together for a few months, but my parents didn't seem to like her much. She lived far away and they didn't want me driving to pick her up. It was mostly my mom. I think my dad would have let me. He didn't think that there was anything wrong with dating. I just think that he believed she wasn't the right person for me.

This went on through the Fall semester. I didn't get to see her as much as I wanted, and so I was frustrated. I tried to figure out what I could do. She and I talked about it as well. Even though we were in the same class, she was a little older than me. After talking it over a few times, we came up with a plan.

### RUNNING AWAY (1984)

The plan that we had come up with was to run away, get married, go to work, and live our lives. Brilliant plan, right? The only reservation I had about that plan was that I didn't want to waste what little time I had left with my dad. But then I thought that I would call him after we settled, and that we could work out something. Again, another brilliant plan.

We ran away at the beginning of the Spring semester and we planned to head for Vancouver, British Columbia. We got up into Oregon and somehow got the idea to turn south and go to Disneyland first. I had cleared out my savings for this plan (I wish I still had that account. My dad helped me open it the first day that I could). We ended up going to Disney and had fun for a couple of days.

After Disneyland, we headed down to the town that I lived in when my family and I had lived in Southern California. The plan was to see my old friend whom I made when I was in third grade. It was easy enough to find him, but there was a problem: I was 16 (almost 17) and I didn't want his parents calling the police on me because I wasn't supposed to be there.

I guess that I could have just told him that my parents had let us come down for a week and that I had stopped by to see him, but I didn't think of that then. So, I just told him that I was a little over a year older than I actually was and that I had already graduated high school. That lie has always bothered me. I'm not one to lie, and I'd like to set the record straight. Anyway, that's another story and there might be more on that later.

We headed back to Canada and drove through Northern Nevada again. The sheriff's department found us sleeping in the car and I went to juvenile hall. I spent the night in holding. I wasn't scared, but I sure didn't like it. My parents came and got me in the morning. I had a hearing in front of a judge a few days later. Nothing much happened, and my parents were given the responsibility to handle the situation. They all agreed that I was not to have any contact with my girlfriend anymore. I now knew that this was never going to work with us attending the same school. I knew I'd wind up in trouble somehow and so would she. So, I asked my parents if I could transfer to the local public school where most of my friends went because I was still at the parochial high school.

## SWITCHING HIGH SCHOOLS (1984)

In just a few days my parents decided that I could transfer to the local public high school. After running away, I had never returned to the other school. When I started at my new school, I had a different set of classes and no religion class. While I enjoyed some of the classes, everything seemed harder. I had to wonder about that because the parochial school was supposed to be the hardest in the area and the only college preparatory school in the region. I had decent grades at this point in high school, but there was a dip at the new school. Another plus to this new school was that many of my friends (aka, "acquaintances") were there. I have pretty much lost contact with everyone from that time in my life.

Not long after transferring, another student transferred over from my previous school. This was a classmate with whom I had gotten into a fistfight and I had survived disciplinary action. He, however, had not. I guess that he learned his lesson because he told everyone at the new school that they should give me a wide berth. From that point on, I had a lot of people coming up to me saying that they would back me up if the need ever were to arise. That was cool, but I've always been the lone wolf. I wound up defending a couple of friends when others tried to start something with them, but I picked and chose those situations. Other than that, I did get that wide berth that my former schoolmate suggested I deserved.

After transferring to the new school, I hooked up with my old girlfriend. Unfortunately, she had transferred to another local school but across town. We had our ups and downs throughout high school, but we always seemed to come back to each other. There was just something about her, and not the least of it was that she was beautiful.

## SIBLING #4 (THE BIRTH OF MY YOUNGEST SISTER)

During this time (unbeknownst to me) my youngest sister was born. She was born in the Winter of 1983-1984. This is the youngest of my four siblings and the one that may be the most like me. It's hard to imagine life with a sibling, or a bunch of siblings, during these times. I wish I had had the opportunity to know these people long before I did. Maybe we would have different relationships now. But then maybe we wouldn't. I just wish that the choice would have been mine and not someone that didn't even care what happened to me.

Life is all about choices, right until you have no choices. I know many people have limited choices in their lives, but you usually don't have to worry about the choice being made to give you away. I would never have chosen what happened to me. I know some adoptees feel that the choice to give them up was for the best. Under different circumstances that could have been true for me. But it wasn't.

## Finishing High School (1985)

While the remainder of high school was uneventful, there were the ups and downs that I mentioned my girlfriend and I were having. Those ups and downs resulted in my having relationships with two other people during that final year and a half of high school. One of these relationships was casual and the other was a little more serious. The only problem with either of these was that I couldn't get my former girlfriend out of my thoughts. I sometimes wonder what I could have done to have a different outcome. It's probably all a waste of time, but maybe it will help me with decisions in the future.

The young lady with whom I had a casual relationship was a former classmate at my previous school. I can't recall how we stayed in touch, but we did. At the new high school, a couple of the classes that I took were

Junior Reserve Officers Training Corps (JROTC). In the late Spring of my first year at the new school, there was the annual military ball. My girlfriend and I had broken up, so I invited my former classmate to the ball with me. It was a nice evening, and I am pretty sure we had dinner at her family's restaurant. We then enjoyed the ball. Afterward, we kept in touch for a while, but we never went out again. The last I heard (from my mom), was that she was working in a doctor's office. I wound up going to a doctor in that office but I never saw her.

I am not sure how my relationship started with the other person that was a little more serious, but it was another time when my girlfriend and I broke up. One thing I will never forget is that she and I had the same birthday: not just the date but the year as well. I don't recall much of what we did but I do remember spending the night at her apartment on our eighteenth birthday. Her mom did not have a problem with this, and I thought that was cool. I recall my mom telling me to be home by 10:00 p.m. The next day when I got home after school, my mom wasn't too happy. Again, what happened slips my mind.

A couple of months later, it was time for graduation. I remember at one point in that semester I wasn't sure I'd be graduating; I was failing English. I got some help with the class from my current girlfriend: the one that shared my birthday. Whatever we did to get that grade up worked. I wound up graduating with a 3.33 GPA which might not sound too bad but it barely put me in the top half of the class. And when I say barely, there were over 300 students in my class, and I was only one or two places from being in the bottom half of the class.

After graduation, I spent the Summer working at a golf course and dating my former girlfriend. I wasn't sure what my next step was, but I applied to the local university and was accepted.

### Tips for Adoptees
#### Know Which Type of Adoption you Are in

- *An Open Adoption is when adoptive and biological parents keep in contact and know each other's information. It can be relatively easy to find your birth parents in this type of adoption, because your adoptive parents know and communicate with your birth parents. The level of communication varies, and it is sometimes possible that the parties lose touch for a variety of reasons.*

- *A Semi-open Adoption is when parents keep in touch through a third party, such as an adoption agency. Adoptive parents usually only have non-identifying information. If your adoptive parents are open to you communicating with your birth parents, they would contact them to see if they wanted contact.*

- *A Closed Adoption is when information is not shared between parties. Some states have closed adoptions, and the only way to contact birth parents is if you both sign*

up for a national or state registry. Both parties must be
signed up in the same registry.

- A Foster Care Adoption would likely be closed, although
  it could be Semi-open or even Open, depending on the
  circumstances.

# CHAPTER 6
# The Selfish Gene

### RIGHT AFTER HIGH SCHOOL

*Modern man thinks he loses something—time—*
*when he does not do things quickly. Yet he does not*
*know what to do with the time he gains—except kill it.*

### ERICH FROMM

### STARTING UNIVERSITY (1985)

I started at the local university in the Fall of 1985. Probably thinking that it would help me in my plans to inherit my dad's business, I studied mechanical engineering. I quickly learned that the math required for the degree was beyond what I wanted to do. I am sure I could have taken the remedial classes to get up to speed and be successful, but that wasn't what I wanted. While I am not bad at math, I was a little unprepared because I hadn't taken the highest levels in high school.

I also took classes in Reserve Officers Training

Corps (ROTC), hoping that I would join the Army as an officer when I did join. I did join, but not as an officer. I spent too much time during the semester screwing around with my girlfriend and not spending enough time studying. When all was said and done, my semester GPA was below 1.00. As a result, I was suspended from the university. Trying to figure out what my next step was, there were two things I was certain that I wanted to do. First, I wanted to marry my girlfriend. Second, I wanted to join the military.

My school failure was paired with yet another event that proved devastating to me. An event with which I felt left with no choices, and it further changed my life forever. Sometime before or during that last semester of school, my girlfriend became pregnant. We discussed the situation and both agreed that the child was mine. I talked to her about getting married and supporting her, probably by joining the Army. Unfortunately, she was 17 at the time and ended up discussing the situation with her mother. I'm not sure which it was, but either her mother forced or convinced her to have an abortion.

You might ask why this was devastating, but I believe the reason is clear. Knowing that I was adopted meant that I knew of no one related to me by blood. This child would have been the first person who I would have known who was related to me by blood. Aside from that, I wanted to be a responsible adult, and there is no way I would give up a child or make this decision if the choice were mine.

I am not here to have the abortion debate. If it were truly her choice and she didn't care about my opinion, I would respect that. However, that isn't the way the situation shook out. We stayed together for a short while but broke up again not long after.

## STARTING COMMUNITY COLLEGE (1986)

The semester after my low GPA, I didn't have the choice to return to school for the Spring. The option for someone in this predicament was to attend the local community college. You have to jump through hoops in order to return to the university, and I hoped that I could get myself squared away. But that wasn't how things happened. My ex-girlfriend and I started talking again. One thing led to another, and the next thing you know we were back together.

Let me tell you, life can get complicated. That Spring semester at the community college didn't go as expected. I had signed up for two classes, and not too long after the semester started, I withdrew.

## HISTORICAL EVENT # 8 (THE CHALLENGER DISASTER)

On January 28, 1986, the Space Shuttle Challenger exploded not long after takeoff. I remember watching the launch, but I'm not sure if I had been watching it live or heard about the explosion and tuned into the news. Looking back, my memory plays tricks on me and I recall this happening when I was in the eighth grade.

I am not sure what to say about this event. Aside from the shock we felt as individuals and a nation, it was hard to believe that we had lost seven astronauts with the advances we had made in technology.

The Space Shuttle Missions were exciting, and I always tried to catch what I could of them on the television and in the news. I never take the loss of life lightly. Those astronauts were someone's family. Not having a biological family increases the pain and distress of seeing people lose their own families. Of course, none of this changes the affection I have for my adoptive family. They have always been there for me, and I won't ever forget that.

## TIPS FOR ADOPTEES
### *HOW TO FIND SOMEONE IF YOU HAVE SOME OF THEIR INFORMATION. MOST IMPORTANTLY, A NAME*

- *There are numerous online sites that allow a person to look up information on other people: sites such as True People Search (TPS), Spokeo, TruthFinder, Whitepages, etc. People can be found with as little as a name. But the more information you have, the easier the search becomes. Remember, there is always that one person who you might never find.*

- *Social Media like Facebook, Twitter, and Instagram among others.*

- *Good-old-fashioned phone books, newspapers, marriage and divorce records, birth and death records, census data, and even military records. Some of this can be found online, and some might require digging. There is always the possibility that you might need to pay for the information.*

Good old-fashioned phone books, newspapers, marriage and divorce records, and death records, com-
are date and even the state records. Some of this can be
found online, and for other things, maybe dig into, there is
always the possibility that you, in need to pay for the
information.

## Chapter 7
# The Making of the Fittest
### United States Army

*Life began, then was done,*
*now I stare into a cold empty well.*

STEVIE WONDER

### First Marriage (1986)

In early April 1986, my girlfriend and I were still together in an off-and-on-again relationship. Being "on
again", I finally convinced her that we should get married. I had already enlisted in the Army earlier in the
Spring, though I was on the Delayed Entry Program (I
was to wait almost 18 months for an opening in Military Police). So, we wasted no time and got married
in April.

I was unemployed at the time and appealed to my recruiter to see if there was a way to move up my enlistment date. He informed me that I could move the date
up, but I would have to select a new Military Occupa-

tional Specialty (MOS). I had to travel to Sacramento to get the change authorized and was offered several different MOS's to choose from if I wanted to leave soon. I chose Infantry and am glad that I did. There isn't much in the world that I am prouder of than my service as an Infantryman.

## BASIC TRAINING (1986)

On the night of May 19, 1986, my parents drove me down to Oakland, California, and we spent the night in a hotel. The next morning, they dropped me off at the Military Entrance Processing Station (MEPS). This was the first time in my life that I recall seeing my dad cry, and it was probably the last.

I took the oath that morning and a group of us were dropped off at San Francisco International in the afternoon for a late flight to Atlanta, Georgia. We arrived in Atlanta late in the evening and were told to assemble in a waiting area for the buses.

We met other recruits in the waiting area, people who came from other locations. The bus arrived sometime around 2:00 a.m. ("0200"). The sun hadn't come up yet when we arrived at Fort Benning, Georgia, and the Sergeant told us that we could get some sleep. It wasn't but a couple of hours later that they woke us up to start in-processing.

"In processing" took us about three days. We were issued uniforms, met the finance people so we could get paid, got haircuts, and got shots. The shots were "fun."

When I got my shots, the next thing I remember was someone waving smelling salts in my face. I had hit the floor right away. Several fellow recruits began to size me up, thinking that I must be the weakest link.

The night of the first day was hard for me. I left the squad bay and went into the hallway. I spent some time there crying because I knew that the chances of my dad being alive when I finished my enlistment were slim. I got all my crying out that day then put those thoughts behind me. I knew I had to man up and get through basic and whatever came next. After all, this is what I wanted to do: serve my country like most men in my family had done.

There were a few memorable moments during basic training. The first was getting off the cattle car that transported us everywhere (or everywhere we didn't walk). The Drill Sergeants were yelling at us, telling us that we had five seconds to get out of the cattle car and that four of them were already gone. They call this the "Shark Attack."

The next memorable thing was that I was not in shape and the physical training was harder than I had imagined it would be. I soon got better at running and sit-ups, but push-ups weren't happening for me. By the end of basic I was one of the fastest runners and could max out the sit-ups, but I just squeaked by on the pushups. I wouldn't find out for years that a heart problem caused my arms not to get a rich supply of oxygenated blood.

Just a few weeks into training the First Sergeant came

to our training area, asking for me. I knew that something was wrong and I was hoping that I wasn't going to be told that my dad had died. When I got back to our company area, I was told to report to the Commanding Officer (CO). When I went in, he told me to have a seat and informed me that my grandfather had died. He asked if I wanted to take the time to go to the funeral. He also told me that if I did, I would be "recycled". That meant that I would have to start basic all over again.

I told him that my grandfather had served on D-Day at the beaches in Normandy and that his advice for me would be to skip the funeral and continue training. The CO asked if that meant I was *not* going to the funeral.

"Yes, sir," I replied. "I am not going to the funeral."

A few weeks later, I ran into another issue. We were almost through the basic training part of our training, and I came down with pneumonia. I spent a number of days in the base hospital.

One morning, I was told that I would be recycled if I didn't return to my unit that day.

"Fuck it," I said and returned to my unit that afternoon, still very sick. Somehow, I recovered over the next few days.

My time in the base hospital was crazy.

First, I saw someone from jump school who had gotten the parachute lines wrapped around his bicep. His arm was filleted with the skin and muscles off the bone. I could see his humerus.

Second, I was taking ice baths several times a day to reduce my temperature. I felt like I was burning up and freezing at the same time.

Our basic training was what is called One Station Unit Training (OSUT) which means that you complete basic and Advanced Individual Training (AIT) at the same time and at the same base. We even stayed in the same barracks for three weeks of training for AIT. All along, I was a member of 2nd Platoon, Bravo Company, 2nd Battalion, 2nd Infantry Training Brigade, Harmony Church at Fort Benning, Georgia. I trained as a Heavy Anti-Armor Weapons Infantryman: MOS 11H. The training was much different from basic, and we trained most of the time between breakfast and dinner.

I knew that my parents were coming for graduation. I might have even told them to come a day early to see if we could visit. They did come and the CO let me see them for a few minutes. I had never been happier to see my dad, and he was so proud of me. It is a moment I will never forget, and it brings a tear to my eye every time I think about it: even right now. I had never been prouder of him either, knowing that the trip wasn't easy for him.

During the time that I was at basic, my wife spent time in a small coastal Oregon town, living with her grandmother. I believe she enjoyed that time. Occasionally, I would be allowed to call home. I know I called my parents a time or two, but most of my calls were to my wife. I missed her a lot and the time away from her was especially hard. I also wrote a few letters home to my parents and even more to my wife.

My wife and mom also sent me letters. I have no idea what happened to them, but I wish that I still had those. I recently discovered a letter I wrote to my parents. It was odd when I found it because my memory of that time has faded. There are guys who remember their roster numbers, the serial number of their basic training M-16 rifle, and other things. But I don't. However, the letter had my social security number and my roster number in the return address. I found it strange that we were sending mail back then with our social security numbers on them!

After graduation, my parents had snapped a few pictures, some of which I also recently found. I met a guy at basic who we called Ibo. His full name was Ferdinand Ibabao.

Ibo was a good friend at basic, one of the few who just tried to do the right thing and survive just as I did. Ibo was assigned to a different company once we got to our permanent duty station. Around 2018 I found out that Ibo was one of the individuals killed in the October 2004 Green Zone Bombing in Baghdad, Iraq. After doing some more research, I learned that he had served six years in the infantry and another six years as Military Police (MP) for the United States Army and Army Reserve. After leaving the Army he was a police officer in Guam before becoming a third-party contractor for the Department of State, providing Diplomatic Security in Iraq.

One of the pictures I recently found was a picture of Ibo next to me at basic training graduation. I didn't even know that I had that picture in my possession, but it is one of my most treasured possessions. I think of Ibo every day. As far as I am concerned, he is a hero even though I am pretty sure he wouldn't feel that way.

Ibo was the best friend that I had at basic, and my only friend. During our first week of training, Ibo and I were both chosen for leadership positions. I was a squad leader, and he was the platoon guide. Squad leaders managed their squads, and the platoon guide was the liaison between the entire platoon and the Drill Sergeants.

I lasted a week as a squad leader because I was a manager, meaning I gave orders and expected others to do what they were told. Ibo was a leader, someone who just led by example and didn't give orders. For a recruit position, Ibo had the right style and I didn't. It is easy to see why I got fired.

Most people didn't like me because I tried to imitate the Drill Sergeants' style. Ibo lasted the entire cycle as platoon guide. He was the only person who treated me well. Everyone else hated me. When we did hand-to-hand and pugil stick training, the Drills said that we could dispose of rank and fight anyone we wanted. A few people wanted to fight me. I agreed to fight all comers, with the condition that it be one-on-one. After the first one, no one else wanted anything to do with that. Little did these recruits know, but this kid from an upper-middle-class family had about four years of training in American Kenpo.

## HAWAI'I DEPLOYMENT &
## THE 25TH INFANTRY DIVISION (LIGHT) 1986-1988

Upon returning home from basic training, I met my wife who had just come back from Oregon. Because I was given a couple weeks of leave, we stayed at my parents' new house which was the first time I had stayed in that house. My dad had just finished building it while I was at basic. We enjoyed our time before heading to Hawai'i. If I recall correctly, we went to Tahoe a few times. I can't remember, but I think my wife's parents (or maybe mine) drove us to San Francisco to fly out a day earlier than expected because I wanted to get to Hawai'i and get a lay of the land before reporting for duty. We got to check into the hotel where we stayed until we found housing a day early. The following day, all the other married couples arrived. I wound up being friends with a few of them, but there was one couple with which my wife and I exclusively spent time.

Many of us couples settled into an apartment complex on the North Shore. We would have to get up super early to make it to daily physical training, but that was fine by us. After a few weeks, our battalion went to the field for at least a week to go through the Light Fighters course which was infantry training for light infantry units. My wife didn't like it much when I went to the field, and we were gone at least a week or more once a quarter. Each passing trip left my wife less than happy with me. After a while, she decided that she wanted to return to Northern Nevada.

Our battalion spent a three-week field training exercise (FTX) at the Pōhakuloa Training Area (PTA) on the Big Island of Hawai'i. I believe that this was after my wife returned to the mainland. I worked 24/7 while at PTA. For the most part, I was assigned as a support driver delivering supplies, food, and ammo to the units of my battalion. I did spend a few days with the TOW Platoon which was a platoon of heavy anti-armor weapons Infantrymen. TOW stood for the weapon system: (T)ube Launched, (O)ptically Tracked, (W)ire-guided heavy anti-tank missile. I might have averaged two hours of sleep each night, and I drove most of the time. I remember getting my only shower during the entire training time just a few days before we returned to O'ahu.

Our other big training exercise was to Subic Bay, Philippines, for Balikatan '87. We flew there on a C5A Galaxy which is one big-ass plane. We had two Huey Helicopters, a couple of five-ton trucks, a few HMMWVs that filled the cargo area, and about 300 troops in the above cargo seating area. The seats were behind the wings and faced the rear.

We had to refuel in Guam. We landed at the U.S. Naval Air Station Cubi Point and spent our time in the Marine Corps Quonset Hut Barracks. As with PTA, I was assigned as a support driver. We got to go into the magazine area to load up rounds for everything from the M-16 to mortars. This required a security clearance which was common for drivers and radio-telephone operators. I earned an Army Achievement Medal for my driving which was presented by an undersecretary of the Army at a Division formation.

I spent most of my time in Hawai'i as a company clerk. Think Radar O'Reilly (but I'm no Radar). I was into computers at the time and used my computer in the office to prepare reports and orders, keeping everything organized. I met a Staff Sergeant (SSG) who was the company Training NCO during this time. We worked hand-in-hand in the office, making sure that our company ran smoothly. He was moved to another position after a while, and I was the acting Training NCO for a time before moving to the support platoon.

I found my Sergeant on Facebook just a couple of years ago and visited him in Arkansas in the Summer of 2021. It was a good meeting. We ate some barbecue and had some beers. I had planned to visit him again last summer, but his wife had just had an accident and he needed to focus his time and efforts on her recovery. I am planning a trip to see him later this year.

I carried out whatever duties I was assigned and didn't complain (not that one could complain). I was disappointed that I didn't get to serve my time in the TOW Platoon, but that is the way it goes. Part of my driving and support duties included a month-long stint supporting the television show *Tour of Duty*. At first I drove producers around, scouting locations in the East Range. Later, I would bring supplies out to the production. Most of the stars from the first season would chat with me from time to time. They were as interested in what I did in the Army as I was in what they did as actors and I had lunch with many of them several times.

I had a few lunches with Terence Knox who played 'Zeke' Anderson the Platoon Sergeant. Another time I tried to have lunch with guest star Tim Thomerson who had starred in the movie *Trancers*, a movie I enjoyed. I told a couple of the stars my intention and they told me to skip it because Thomerson went deep into his roles and refused to be bothered. I watched him study his lines across the road from where a group of us ate. It was interesting.

Other than following my orders, I spent my time off either at the beach on North Shore (mostly at Waimea Bay) or drinking in the evenings in Waikiki.

I did a lot of drinking after my wife left, but I also enjoyed some time with an ex-high school girlfriend who flew over for a week. She had joined the Army Reserve and caught a Military Airlift Command (MAC) flight for ten dollars. We enjoyed time on the North Shore. I asked her to stay when her time was up but she had to return home. I asked her if she would marry me once my divorce was final but she was not interested—although we have remained friends. Sometimes, I wish things had been different between us. I would see her a few times after that.

A couple of things happened while being married and having my ex-girlfriend from high school come for a visit. First, I found out that my wife's father was not her biological father. Second, I found out that my ex-girlfriend was adopted as well.

I don't know if I know all the details about my ex-girl-friend, but I do know those of my wife. I received a call one day at our apartment, and a man asked for my wife. I asked who he was, and he said he was her father. I told him that was impossible because I knew her dad and he wasn't him. He explained that he was her biological father and that the man I knew had adopted her when he married her mother. It's interesting to me how many instances of adoption come up, especially for someone who is adopted.

## THE DIVORCE ("I'M NOT COMING BACK")

I mentioned that my wife left Hawai'i to return home. I also mentioned that she did not like it when I was in the field. It turned out that while I was in the field, she was hanging out with another soldier from the division. Some other things were going on with her, too.

When she decided to leave, all I could do was take her to the airport and say goodbye. At the time, I didn't know if she was going to come back or not because she wouldn't tell me if she was leaving for good. Shortly after her return home, we spoke, and she told me that she was not returning. I told her that we should get a divorce and she agreed.

I had my parents find me a lawyer back home and I got the process going. Because we didn't own any property and we didn't have any kids, it was a simple process. Before I knew it I had the official divorce decree and our time together was over.

## LOSS #3 (DAD'S DEATH)

In March of 1988 most of the battalion went on a stateside deployment to Fort Lewis, Washington. I was chosen as part of a small cadre to stay in Hawai'i. It wasn't too many days after the battalion departed that I was summoned to the office by the executive officer. That day, I had walked back and forth from the motor pool for lunch. The walk took a little while. When I returned to the motor pool after lunch, I received a summons to the office. I knew that something was wrong because there was no reason to be summoned.

When I arrived at the office, the executive officer told me that my dad had a heart attack and it didn't look like he was going to make it. Orders were cut for me to return to the mainland, and my unit investigated how I would return. There wasn't a MAC flight scheduled anytime soon that would get me to where I needed to go, so I was booked on a United flight.

I arrived at LAX the next day, and my uncle (the Vietnam Vet) picked me up to drive me out to where my dad had a heart attack. I remember him telling me that I needed to be strong for the family, especially for my mom.

When I got to the location, I saw my dad and met my mom. We stayed there for a couple of days while my dad was in the cardiac ICU. On the fourth day, my mom and I went to lunch at a restaurant nearby. The nurses had told us that they would call if anything happened. When we returned, they told us they had been trying to call but that my dad had died while we were gone. We went to the hotel, packed our bags, and headed back to Northern Nevada.

The next day, we planned with a local funeral home to have my dad's remains transported home. He arrived within a day or so. We had a viewing, a Catholic Burial Mass, and then a graveside gathering. My mom didn't want the flag draped over his coffin, so I requested that it just be placed on it, already folded. When the graveside gathering was just about over, I presented my mom with the flag and gave her the thanks of a grateful nation for his service in the Navy during World War II.

I had brought my dress uniform and dress blues. I ended up wearing the blues for the funeral. My uncle appreciated my taking the place of a graveside detail. I got through all of it with no external shows of emotion, but I was dying inside.

Afterward, I called my ex-girlfriend who had visited Hawai'i and asked if I could come to see her. I told her about my dad, and she agreed. I wound up staying at her apartment for several days. I did a lot of crying during that time, and she was there with me through most of it.

Once my emergency leave came to an end, my mom asked if there was any way that I could stay. I went and talked to my recruiter who suggested that I contact my unit and request a compassionate transfer to somewhere stateside that would be close to home. The unit responded that they would investigate the matter. But in the meantime, I was cut temporary orders to serve at the recruiting office.

After a little over three months, the word came back that I was going to be separated from the service with a compassionate discharge. This wasn't what I wanted, but it was what was offered. In July I went to Oakland, California, and I was processed out of the Army.

## TIPS FOR ADOPTEES
### *DNA Testing*

- *Without information about your birth family from your adoptive family or your Original Birth Certificate, DNA testing is your best bet.*

- *As mentioned at the end of Chapter 2, the best testing sites are Ancestry, 23andMe, and MyHeritage. If you can afford more than one, it could be wise to do so. Wait for results from Ancestry before testing at 23andMe, and the same if testing with the third site.*

- *If you find a Parent match, read the information at the end of Chapters 12, 13, and 14. Also, use the information included at the end of the previous chapter. While it might be easy to direct message the Parent, it might not be the wisest idea. In the end, the decision is yours.*

# CHAPTER 8
# The Third Chimpanzee

## ARMY RESERVE, RESERVE DEPUTY SHERIFF & CORRECTIONAL OFFICER

*There are two tragedies in life.*
*One is to lose your heart's desire.*
*The other is to gain it.*

### GEORGE BERNARD SHAW

### SECOND MARRIAGE (1988)

During my time at the recruiting office, I tried to convince my ex-girlfriend (the one who visited me in Hawai'i) to give it a go again. I also spent some time with my ex-wife trying to see if we could patch things up. It probably wasn't the best decision, trying to convince two different women to have a relationship with me.

I spent a lot of time in the evenings, especially on Friday and Saturday nights, cruising the main drag in town. There was another soldier assigned to the recruiting office who was also a "compassionate." I had a Pontiac Firebird at the time and he had a Chevrolet Camaro. He would go cruising, too, and we would go out for drinks as well.

One night while out cruising, I kept seeing this girl who was cruising as well. I kept trying to catch up with her, but she was always on the other side of the street. I saw her again another night and we finally met up in the parking lot of a casino. I got her phone number and told her that I would give her a call. For several days I didn't call her because I couldn't find the number. I wound up finding the number and gave her a call. We soon began dating and having a good time.

Before I knew it, I asked her if she would like to get married and she said yes. We got married not too long after that, which was before I reported to Oakland for out-processing.

## ARMY RESERVE (1988-1992)

Not long after getting married and out-processing, I stopped in the recruiting office to see my friend, the SSG who had recruited me. He introduced me to their new Army Reserve recruiter. The recruiter and I talked, and she told me about the reserve units in the area. I decided to join the medical unit that operated out of the Veterans Administration (VA) hospital. The recruiter told me that I did not have to sign a contract because I had served on active duty and already had one. She also told me that I was not required to be in the Active Reserve (AR). Also, if I chose not to continue, I would just be placed back in the Individual Ready Reserve (IRR).

I went for a couple of months and knew that I didn't want to be a medic. One reason I chose the medical unit was because that was the unit my ex-girlfriend was in at the time. I told the commanding officer (CO) that the unit wasn't working out for me. He told me that it was no problem. He knew that I didn't have a contract for Active Reserve and that I could go back to the IRR anytime I wanted. He released me with no issues.

## COMMUNITY COLLEGE (SECOND TIME AROUND) 1988

During the Fall of 1988, I returned to community college and started working on a criminal justice degree. I did well in a couple of classes, not too bad in another, and withdrew from my fourth class. At the end of the semester I didn't sign up for classes for the following Spring. I was working and didn't have a lot of money to spare (not that school cost me anything with the G.I. Bill), but I needed the money from my job to pay my other bills and didn't think that I would fare well working and going to school full time. I knew that I wanted to get a degree, but I just didn't know how I would do it.

The other worry on my mind was that my dad was gone. I struggled with that a lot. He was the greatest man whom I had ever known. I loved him very much, but he was gone and there was a hole in my heart.

## Reserve Deputy Sheriff & Correctional Officer (1988-1990)

During this time I had put in a few applications for a law enforcement position. I wound up testing for the Douglas County Sheriff's Department. I was in good physical shape, shot well, and answered all the questions right. As I recall, over 1,000 applicants were competing for one open position. By the time the backgrounding was done, only about 500 remained qualified. Out of those I had done the best on the firing range and quite well in other areas.

There was a short list of applicants of which number one was hired and the rest were placed on the waiting list for any positions that might come up soon. I believe that the department averaged one hire a year. I was number three on the list which became number two once the number one applicant took the open position.

A few months later, I wound up applying for a position as a correctional officer for the Department of Prisons. I didn't know how long the wait would be at the Sheriff's Office and I needed a better job than the one that I had. Once I was placed on the list at the Sheriff's Office, I was offered a part-time, non-paid position as a Reserve Deputy. I had to complete their reserve academy which gave me a Level 3 Peace Officers Standards and Training (POST) Certificate. After a while, I was offered a position with the Department of Prisons, and I left my Reserve Deputy position.

I went through the Prison's Level 3 POST academy and went to Ely, Nevada to work at the new maximum-security prison. I spent time on death row, in the administrative segregation unit, and as the culinary officer, as well as training for their Special Operations and Response Team (SORT): the prison version of a SWAT Team.

Not long after getting to Ely, I found out that my wife was having an affair with another correctional officer. I requested a transfer to Carson City and filed for a divorce. I also left the prison after a time because of a dispute with one of my superiors. He didn't like me because I was acquainted with several ex-inmates. I was only acquainted with them because they had been former customers at a convenience store where I worked. When asked on my application if I knew any ex-inmates, in an attempt at transparency I listed these individuals. I explained the situation when I was hired and the committee was fine with it.

But this one superior was on the committee, and he held it against me. He always assigned me to crappy postings and shifts. I didn't like the circumstances I left under, but I was glad to be gone. I attempted to get my Reserve Deputy position back, but I burned the bridge there when I left for the prisons.

## THE FOREIGN AFFAIR ("IT'S OVER")

Not long after leaving the prisons, I returned to the convenience store industry. I was spending some weekend evenings out having fun dancing at some Country Western bars. During that time I met a young lady and we hit it off. She was from Belgium and liked the Country Western scene. We dated for a while and then she had to return to Belgium for a month to renew her visa.

While she was gone for a month, I was living at her place. Shortly after she returned, she called off our relationship. A few months later, her roommate called and told me that my ex was pregnant and that the child was mine. I asked the roommate how far along she was. The math didn't add up. She was only a couple of months pregnant, and it had been longer than that since we had broken up. I told her my thoughts and she said I was probably right. That was the last that I heard from either of them.

## COMMUNITY COLLEGE (THIRD TIME AROUND) 1990

I started back at community college in the Spring of 1990, registering for two classes. I probably made it through a month of the semester, but I was struggling with work while trying to balance school as well. I withdrew from both of my classes before the withdrawal deadline.

It was around this time that I also started dating another lady. I am sure that didn't help the school situation either.

When registration for the Fall semester opened, I signed up for another couple of classes, hoping that I could figure out how to better schedule my time. Luckily, I did complete both of those classes. This did help to get me on track, but there was still a long road ahead of me.

## THIRD MARRIAGE (1990)

I then met a lady whom an acquaintance had been dating. They were no longer dating, so I asked her out. We went out a few times and she seemed nice enough. I asked my acquaintance if he had a problem with us dating, and he said no.

After a while, I thought things were going well. I liked her because she was older and I thought she had her head screwed on right while most of the women my age did not. Once I came to this conclusion, I asked her to marry me, hoping that this would be the last time I got married. She said yes, and not too long after that we were married. This was near the end of August 1990.

## HISTORICAL EVENT #9 (THE GULF WAR)

Right before we got married, the United States started sending troops to the Middle East in preparation for a potential invasion of Iraq. Iraqi forces had invaded Kuwait. I was in the Reserve currently and was training to reclassify from Infantryman to Chemical Operations Specialist (MOS 54B). I volunteered to be sent to the Middle East because of my expertise in chemical operations.

But my reserve unit would not release me for an assignment because I was still in the middle of training and they hadn't been called to be activated. Several of my fellow soldiers who were going through training were called up to join Operation Desert Shield (Desert Shield was the codename for the buildup in the Gulf).

Those individuals didn't finish their MOS training. But since I was not allowed to go, I did finish mine and was the Honor Graduate of the class. There were a couple of other people who might have been the Honor Graduate, but I edged them out in the end, continuing to pass all the tests with the highest grade.

My Commanding Officer didn't think I would pass my school, and I told him that I would return as the honor graduate. At the same time when the Gulf War was imminent, I volunteered to join our forces in the Middle East. With my Commanding Officer's lack of confidence in me, his unwillingness to allow me to put in for combat duty, his refusal to release me for a position as an instructor at the 54B School with the California National Guard, and the birth of my daughter, I decided to leave the Reserves. My Commanding Officer didn't think that I could just leave. He thought I had a contract like a regular Reserve enlistee which

I didn't. He illegally reduced me in rank, but I didn't care. My time in the military was over. If they didn't need me, then I didn't need them.

## Offspring #1 (The Birth of My Oldest Daughter)

Without my knowledge my oldest daughter was born in the middle of September 1990. This was just weeks after I was married again and had volunteered to go to the Middle East. Had I known that I had a child and had I been allowed in her life, I probably would not have volunteered to join Desert Storm.

It is one thing to take risks when it is only me (or even just me and my wife), but I would never want a child of mine to grow up without me being there. And I never got to make that choice. In this case my daughter would grow up without me, not knowing that I existed until she was 12 and not meeting me until she was an adult. None of this was my choosing, and it never would be.

That is not who I am.

### Tips for Adoptees
*What to Do with Your Matches on a DNA Site*

- *Shared DNA is measured in centimorgans (cM's). Matches of 225 cM's and above can be quite useful for locating a birth parent if no birth parent shows up as a match. 225 cM's is in a range that includes second cous-*

*ins.*

- *If you have any matches that share 225 cM's or more, take screenshots of all their information. If there are more than three or four of these matches, you need only screenshot the top three or four, those with the highest amount of shared DNA. However, I suggest you screenshot all of them.*

- *Unless you have a parent match, or you are very familiar with DNA matches, shared cM's, and analyzing data for a genetic genealogy analysis, I strongly suggest that you find someone to help you with your search.*

# Chapter 9
# On Human Nature
## Blood Is Thicker Than Water

*Blood is thicker than water, but family isn't just about blood. Family is about faith, and loyalty, and who you love. If you don't have those things, I don't care what the blood says. You're not family.*

MIRA GRANT

## University (Second Time Around) & Community College (Fourth Time Around) 1991-1996

In the Summer of 1991 I decided that it was time to get back to school. I registered for two classes at the university and two classes at the community college. With work, school, and early in the semester a new child, school wasn't easy. I did the best that I could but I dropped one of my classes before the semester was over. My GPA at the end of the semester was 2.66: not good but not horrible. I would continue to grind my way through school for many years to come.

OFFSPRING #2
THE BIRTH OF THE FIRST PERSON I EVER KNEW WHO
WAS RELATED TO ME

In September of 1991 my daughter was born. For a
long time to come, she was the only child whom I knew
I had and the only person in the world whom I knew
was related to me. At the age of 24 (after knowing for
12 years that I was adopted), I finally had someone
who I knew was my blood. It was simply amazing to
have someone that close.

I have recently thought that this daughter who was
born in the Fall of 1991 might not feel as connected to
me as she once had. I don't know if this is an accurate
statement but it is something that I occasionally sense.
Things went well between her and her older sister for
a while, but they aren't that way anymore.

My own oldest sister seems to have some resentment
towards me. I don't know if she told me or if someone
else in the family mentioned it, but I believe that she
doesn't like it now that I am the oldest sibling. Maybe
my younger daughter feels that way? These are topics
that I stray away from because I don't want to bring
any bad feelings out of myself or others.

What I can assure is that my younger daughter is
always my first child and that she will always be the
person who made me a dad. She will also always be
the person who was my first blood relative. She holds

a special place in my heart and that will never change. My older daughter is my child as well, but she will never be any of the things that my younger daughter is to me. They both need to know that is alright. Much of that is just the circumstances of our lives that will never change. My children are my children, and I love each one of them in a different way but all as *my* children. There is nothing that can come between my children and me, and anything that tries had better be warned.

The only thing that I cannot do is interfere with their relationships between each other. If they were still kids, then maybe I could. But as adults, it is all up to them. My wish is that they could all get along. There is more to the story, but that is all that I feel I should share. We all deserve our private lives, even after this book is published.

The main point of this chapter is that blood relatives mean the most to me. That is not to say that I don't love those few of my adopted family who are still with us. That also doesn't mean that my brothers and sisters in the military and law enforcement (First Responders) are not important to me. But for me, blood must come first.

## FINAL MARRIAGE

I got married for a fourth time in November 1996. Yes, the mother of my daughter and I had been divorced. I was still working at the same place, and I had been attending school off and on during the years since I last mentioned it. I put together a coed softball team and we were playing in the city league. I knew some of the women on the team and others came to me as referrals from the male players.

One evening, I thought that we might be short a couple of women so I asked if anyone knew someone who could come and fill in for the evening. One of the women whom I had dated a few times brought her roommate with her. It turned out that we did not need any extra players that night.

Afterward we all went to a local bar after the game, and I talked to this friend's roommate. Before the evening was over, I asked her if she would like to go out with me on a date. I don't know if it could be called a date, but we went out to a Country bar and did some dancing. By the time the night was over, I had convinced her that we should go out on a real date.

I am not sure what happened over the next few months, but we spent a lot of time together. I am sure that I asked her to marry me at least 99 times. I would get a "no" each time. But I was sure that this was the person with whom I wanted to be for the rest of my life. This relationship was different from any other I had. I don't really know if it was 99 times that I asked her, but it had to be close. I do know that I must have worn her down because the last time I asked her, the answer was yes.

## Tips for Adoptees
### Finding a Helper (Search Angel)

- *There are a number of free helpers on Facebook in groups such as Search Squad. Find one of these groups and make a post asking for help. They each have a pinned post or something similar that states what information they are looking for. Post as much as possible. If you post screenshots, blackout the names. You can share that directly if you find a Search Angel.*

- *Be warned: not everyone gets a Search Angel. I'd guess that 99.9% of searchers do find a Search Angel, but don't assume that you will get one. This is really about managing your expectations. You might have to post in multiple groups to increase your chances. Once you do have one, let the other groups know you have found one in another group. It's the right thing to do.*

- *Be prepared to give the Search Angel any information that they require. You will need to allow them read-only access to your DNA account (that's the way it's done on Ancestry, and I am not sure how it works on the other sites).*

## CHAPTER 10
# The Mismeasure of Man
### Life in My 30's

*Emotions don't interfere in my acting,*
*nor in my life.*

SIMONA PANOVA

### FINALLY, A DEGREE (1997)

My new wife knew that I had completed all but my mathematics requirement for an associate degree. Looking back on it, it's unfortunate to realize that I had both taken and dropped a math class several times that could have covered the requirement. It wasn't even a high-level math class but only college math. For some reason, math was not clicking with me. I was good at everyday math but could not seem to get a teacher to help who made any sense of it to me. And I didn't have time to get tutoring.

I contacted the college to ask if any other options would meet this requirement. They gave me a few, and I finally enrolled in math for nurses. It wasn't considered a remedial course, but it was one of the lowest-numbered courses that met the requirement. I had it in my mind that this course for medical professionals would be difficult, but I surprised myself by doing well and finishing the course.

I had already walked at graduation a couple of years before I completed this course. Even though it took me several years to complete this course, what is important to me is that I did. I even completed a degree audit just to make sure that completion of the math course would wrap up my degree.

When the semester ended and my grades were posted, I finally had a college degree, earning an Associate of Applied Science in Criminal Justice with an emphasis in Law Enforcement. I was proud of myself and happy that my wife had talked me into it. My wife was proud of me, too.

## Offspring #3 (The Birth of My Son)

Nothing of significance occurred over the next few years. Life went on and we lived our lives. But the Summer of 2000 changed this. My wife became pregnant and we were expecting our first child together.

We went to Southern Nevada to break the news to her parents shortly after we told my mom. My mom wasn't that thrilled about it, and I don't think that my in-laws were either. But my wife had a steady job and was planning for her maternity leave to begin sometime in December. We had planned that she would take a couple of weeks off before the birth and six weeks after. It turned out to be that she had a couple of weeks longer off before the birth because we found out that our son was to be born right around Christmas and he actually came a little late.

January 3, 2001, was when our son decided to arrive. To honor my dad, we gave him my dad's name. We had also decided that he would be born at home and that we would use a midwife instead of the traditional hospital delivery. The only problem with this plan was that we were living with my mom with whom I was assisting with her health issues. We knew that she would not go for a home birth in her house, so we had to find somewhere else.

It turned out that one of my friends was renting a house and was not there often. I convinced him to let us have the birth there and we were set. There was a point, however, when I went out to a convenience store to get some food and the homeowner showed up to the house. She had no idea what my friend had agreed to do. My poor wife had to explain it to her in my absence, and I am sure that was uncomfortable for her.

But our plans continued and the birth went fine. In fact, we returned home within 12 hours. I now had a son, and two people who I knew were related to me. Needless to say, I was excited.

When I say I was very excited, that is an understatement. I mean, I had just doubled the number of people that I knew were related to me! Double—from one to two—might not sound like a lot to many, but it was a whole new world to me. While all of this was overwhelming, I didn't know how to express my feelings about this and still don't.

When someone has an experience that they tell me was fantastic, outstanding, amazing, or whatever, and then they ask me what I think—that's where I get stuck. I *might* feel the same way inside, but my response usually is, "It was good." People get mad at me: "What do you mean *good*? It was *amazing!*"

Like I said, on the inside I am in total agreement. But my external expression doesn't match how I feel. I believe that it comes down to the fact that I have trouble expressing external emotion. There could be many factors for why this is so. It could be from my upbringing, from the time when my dad died and my uncle told me that I had to hold my emotions in. I just don't know.

Suffice it to say that when my son was born, I was internally as excited as all get out. It was the same when my daughter was born. The daughter I knew.

## HISTORICAL EVENT #10 (9/11)

When I was stationed in Hawai'i, I had made several trips to the Arizona Memorial at Pearl Harbor. Even when touring this site, it is hard to imagine the loss of life that occurred there on December 7, 1941: the "day that will live in infamy."

But who would have imagined that approximately 60 years later our nation would be attacked again and that the loss of life would be even greater? This time, we weren't facing a known enemy: one that was state sponsored. We were facing terrorism.

I vividly remember that day, September 11, 2001, and the weeks and years that followed. This one event would lead our nation into its longest period of sustained combat operations. I always imagined that if something like that happened, I would be a part of the fight. However, I had to sit this one out just like a ton of patriotic and restless men of age did. From the comfort of my home.

I was and still am disappointed that I missed the action. While I would have found it extremely difficult to go to war with a ten-year-old daughter and newborn son at home, it would have fulfilled a deep need that I had to be in the fight. Men don't join the infantry to sit at home while their brothers and sisters take the fight to our enemy. We joined to do the job that we signed up for.

Even if I had been able to go as a nuclear, biological, and chemical operations specialist, at least I would have been in the fight. An acquaintance just made me realize that this feeling of regret I experience is called survivors' guilt. Why did I get to sit at home while my brothers and sisters got to do their jobs? Well, that's just the way life shakes out sometimes. I did my job while I was in, and now it is time for others to do theirs.

## COMMUNITY COLLEGE
## FIFTH TIME AROUND (2005)

In the mid-2000s, I decided that it was time to return to school and do my best to earn a bachelor's degree. In an effort to achieve this, I started back at the local community college. I had decided that I wanted to pursue a degree in Anthropology, and my goal was to earn an Associate Degree in Anthropology and then move on to the university.

Once I started taking classes, Murphy's law kicked in again. Before I knew it, something drastic happened that required me to withdraw from college for the remainder of the semester.

## MY CORONARY ARTERY BYPASS SURGERY (2005)

In the Fall of 2005, I went to the doctor for a regular checkup. I had asked for a prescription for Prilosec because I was having what felt like frequent heartburn. My doctor said that he wanted me to get checked out by a cardiologist before he would write me a prescription. I wasn't too thrilled at this prospect, but I set up the appointment.

It took a few weeks to get in, and the cardiologist wanted me to take a stress test. That test was set up and I took it a few days later. While driving home from that appointment, my wife called me and told me that the cardiologist's office called and wanted me to come back to their office immediately. She sounded worried, and that caused me to be a little worried myself.

I returned to the office, and I was told that I had failed the stress test. So, they wanted to set up a heart catheterization procedure. They set this up pretty quickly. The next thing I knew, I was in the hospital for another procedure that was a pretest. That test didn't reveal anything, so I was told that I would keep my appointment for the catheterization.

I went in, had the procedure, and was scheduled to see the doctor the following day. At that appointment, I was told that I had a 90% blockage left anterior descending (LAD) artery. The doctor couldn't tell for sure what the blockage was, but he said that it did not look like anything that he had seen before. To get a better understanding of the blockage, the doctor wanted me to go to Stanford University Hospital to have an ultrasound heart catheterization. That took me right back to the same hospital where my dad had his bypass surgery.

I went a week or two later to Stanford and had the procedure. The report that was sent back to my cardiologist was that the blockage was not caused by any of the usual suspects like cholesterol. The doctor at Stanford reported that this was a *congenital* defect. Basically, I was just born with this narrowing in the artery. My cardiologist referred me to a heart surgeon and I was set up in record time to have bypass surgery. While the surgeon would have preferred to place a stent in me, there was not one big enough at the time to do the job.

My wife tells me that I was in surgery far longer than they estimated and that she was worried when the time ran over so long. However, I recovered quickly and was out of the hospital in 72 hours. Within 30 days, I was back to "normal."

What is ironic is that when I went for my 30-day follow-up, the doctor told me that there was now a stint large enough that I would not have had to have the bypass. Thirty days is the difference between being carved like a Thanksgiving turkey and having a stent placed. Lucky me.

I can imagine how my wife felt when the surgery went longer than expected. Even though my mom and I were told that my dad's open-heart surgery would be very long, the wait was agonizing. There were two main reasons that the surgery went long.

First, the surgeon wanted to test the arteries in my arms for a second time, which means that they were tested once before the surgery and were determined to be worthless for bypass surgery. Apparently, they did not deliver a good flow of oxygen to my arms, and that meant that I couldn't afford to have them used. Also, they probably would not have worked as they should in a bypass procedure.

The second reason the surgery went long was because the surgeon had trouble detaching the mammary artery which was used for the bypass surgery. The doctor would have preferred to bypass the blockage at several points but had to settle for one. Anyway, this is what caused the extra time that made my wife so worried.

And what about me? I just went to sleep and woke up.

## UNIVERSITY (THIRD TIME AROUND) 2006-2008

In the Spring of 2006, I returned to the community college full-time and also started back at the university, taking one class. I had planned to take a class at the university each semester until I earned my associates in Anthropology. That way, I could use the credits for my associates (if they transferred) and be working on the requirements and credits needed to graduate from the university.

It was a good plan and it worked out well for me. It would allow me to graduate sooner once I transferred full-time to the university.

## GETTING MY ASSOCIATE OF APPLIED ANTHROPOLOGY (2006)

After the Fall semester of 2006, I completed all the requirements for my Associates in Applied Anthropology. I worked hard all year in 2006 and it really paid off for me. One thing of note is that the community college only had graduation in the Spring. So I didn't walk in the Fall. When graduation time came along, I think that my mom was proud of me. She wasn't much for complimenting me, so I am not sure though I hope she was.

When I graduated, my family and mom attended. My mom wound up having some breathing issues during the ceremony because of problems with her oxygen tank. She also missed part of the festivities. She was always saying that she was dying when things like this occurred, but it wasn't her time quite yet.

## Tips for Adoptees
### *Important Other Steps*

- *Upload your raw DNA data to GEDMatch. You should find instructions online or in one of the Facebook Groups such as Search Squad.*

- *Also upload your results to other DNA sites that allow it. This info can also be found online or in one of the Facebook Groups such as Search Squad.*

- *Stay proactive and follow the instructions from your Search Angel. They are one of the best resources you'll find. And best of all, they are free.*

## CHAPTER 11

# The Blind Watchmaker

### LIFE IN MY 40'S

*All the people we loved, who have died,
are still alive in the past.*

DIANA PALMER

### RECEIVING MY BACHELOR'S DEGREE (2008)

I kept up the pace that I had started at the community college when I began full-time at the university. I planned to graduate as quickly as possible, and I also planned to earn a master's degree in Anthropology in record time. At least some of that plan worked out.

After graduating from the community college in the Spring of 2007, I graduated from the university with my bachelor's in the Spring of 2008. When I walked, I still had one class to complete to earn my degree. I took an elective class that Summer since I only needed the credits to fulfill my residency requirement. A couple of months after I completed that class, I received my diploma in the mail. While the posting of the degree on one's transcripts is all that matters, having the diploma is nice.

During graduation I had my phone on vibrate so that if anyone texted or called, it wouldn't interfere with graduation. As the ceremony started, I began receiving numerous calls and texts. If I recall correctly, I believe the calls were from both my wife and daughter. I instinctively knew that something was wrong, but I continued on with graduation.

I checked in with my wife right after I walked across the stage. I learned that my mom was having trouble with her oxygen just as she did at my last graduation. Onsite paramedics treated her, and she ended up being fine. This kind of drama was normal in anything involving my mom. That might sound calloused, but it's simply true. She was always fine in the end. She just wanted attention.

## STARTING A MASTER'S DEGREE (2008)

I applied for and was accepted into the master's program for a degree in Cultural Anthropology at the university during the Spring of 2008, and I started classes that Fall. I was an average student. But while I worked hard, I just couldn't seem to get an A to save my life.

However, I did receive an A- during my first semester, and it was in the hardest class of the program. This was a class that other students struggled in, so I was proud of my accomplishment. From this point forward, I just kept grinding away, always doing my best.

## LOSS #4 (FATHER'S DEATH)

As with the other deaths that I learned happened in my birth family's lives, the death of my birth father was no different. It was an event that, quite frankly, I had no clue about.

In March 2010, my birth father passed away at the age of 60. By this time, my mother had lost a husband, my siblings had lost their father, and I had lost the chance to know the man who was my biological father. I think of how much this sucks, but in the end, it is what it is. In other words, it was never meant to be, there is nothing I can do about it, and I have to move on and live my life. You can't change the past, but the past changes you if you can't stop living in it. The irony of the whole situation is that he had open heart bypass surgery the week before and passed due to complications.

Having said that, this is a hard truth for me to live with. If my mother and father didn't want me, that would be one thing. I think that I even could have gotten over that. Oh, how I wish that I could live in the present 100% of the time without worrying about what is past or what is to come. Frankly, I think a lot of people have this problem.

One reason I live some of my life in the past is because I don't ever want to forget all the good things that have happened. But remembering those good things also makes me remember the "other" things. Dreaming about the future is not much different. I dream about how good things could be, but I also dream of how things might not quite work out.

If you are like me in this way, then I feel for you.

## WORKING FOR THE BOY SCOUTS OF AMERICA (2011-2014)

I had been puttering along and working on my master's degree, and my mom had been managing to keep on living despite her health conditions for the past few years. The first real change in a while came along through an opportunity with the Boy Scouts of America (BSA).

I had been volunteering for the BSA since my son was in the first grade. It started out as me being a den leader in his pack, and it continued with me joining the pack leadership and working as a volunteer for both the district and the Nevada Area Council. The executive with whom I worked under decided to take a position at another council. Part of his leaving turned out to be a recommendation that I take his place. He ran it up the chain at the council, and I ended up interviewing to become the District Executive for the area in which I lived which was a paid executive position working for the council.

In the early part of January 2001, I became the District Executive.

## MY DAUGHTER'S PUP (2011)

Sometime during February 2011, my daughter dropped by the house with her new puppy. He was an English Bulldog and he was the cutest little pup I had ever seen.

We decided to go out for a while, and we left him in our entryway to play. When we came back, he had done well and was very excited. I fell in love with that little guy that day and still have a place in my heart for him to this day.

If my heart could take it, and if having a pet was something I wanted to do, I would get myself a little English Bulldog.

## EXITING MY MASTER'S DEGREE (2011)

The Spring semester of 2011 found me making absolutely zero progress on my master's degree. I had finished all my coursework, passed the comprehensive, and was in the third semester of my thesis. I spent those three semesters working on the application for the Institutional Review Board, trying to gain approval to do research with human subjects.

I had the application all prepared for the second semester of thesis and ran it by my chairman. When he got back with me by the end of the semester, he told me that it looked good. I submitted it at the beginning of the next semester and received the response that it was garbage.

Over the Summer I needed to enroll in another thesis class to work on revising the application. The demands of my job, lack of progress in my thesis work, and my mom's declining health led me to finally decide to withdraw from the program. I didn't know if it was the right decision at the time, but it was the one I made.

## HISTORICAL EVENT #11 (AIR RACE DISASTER)

Every September, the Reno International Air Races come to the region. Working for the Boy Scouts, one of the annual fundraisers was operating a parking lot at the event. The Scout Executive and Assistant Scout Executive (CEO & COO) of the Council would work the weekdays because they weren't that busy, and the full executive staff would work the busier weekend. We never made it to the weekend.

On Friday, September 16, 2011, a plane crashed. The pilot and 10 spectators were killed, and a few others were seriously injured. The remainder of the Air Races were canceled, and there was serious doubt if there would ever again be a Reno International Air Race.

Luckily, the Air Races continued the following year, and they have been ongoing since.

## LOSS #5 (MOM'S DEATH)

Shortly before the Air Races at the end of August (or the beginning of September), my mom went into hospice care. She didn't seem any worse than she had for years, but I did not know for sure. She would never allow anyone to go in with her to her doctor's appointments, and the doctors would not provide any information (HIPAA doesn't allow doctors to provide information unless the patient authorizes it). It ended up that she was sicker than I knew and had been taking doses of liquid morphine to manage her pain.

On the morning of September 23, 2011, I worked from home simultaneously trying to get a little time with my mom, though she was totally out of it. I didn't know how much longer she had.

I headed off to work in the afternoon and left her with someone at home to watch her. Before I got to work, however, the young lady watching her called to tell me that she had died. All I could think was that she had finally done it and died like she had been saying she would every day for the last 10-plus years.

It was horrible to lose my last remaining parent, but she was no longer in pain. I was also relieved, knowing that I could finally live my life the way I wanted to live it without my mother telling me what to do or questioning every one of my decisions. In a way I was at peace, too.

While I pretty much lost my childhood when my mom told me that I was adopted and carried that burden well into adulthood before I found my birth family, this moment might have been the first time that I was really an adult. No matter what I did, my mom was always right there meddling in my affairs and trying to get me to do things just the way she wanted. I would ask her advice on occasion, but I never felt like my life was my own. With her death my life was finally my own. Life with her really was hell in retrospect.

That didn't mean that her dying was not upsetting to me or that I wouldn't miss her. But maybe hell was over.

## WILDFIRE (2011)

November 2011 saw my family and me evacuating our house due to a late-season wildfire. I am always worried about losing my home because it is the last house that my father built. It holds some memories for me as well as a few of my dad's. But its real value is that it was built by his hand and those of his crew.

We gathered up as many of our personal belongings, important papers, and other possessions as we could carry in our vehicles. When all was safe, we returned, but many of our neighbors weren't that lucky.

Several houses in our neighborhood burned to the ground, and those families lost everything. This was a very stressful time having left school, experiencing the Air Races accident, losing my mom, and having to evacuate because of the fire.

## Loss #6 (Brother's Death)

December 17, 2012, was just another day for me. However, it was not another day for my mother. Not only had she lost her firstborn to adoption three days after my birth, but she lost her only other son when my brother passed away that day. As I mentioned before, my parents had not made me the III, but named my younger brother the III. That had to have been hard for her.

I wonder if they thought of me when this happened. I can't even describe how much I love my sisters, but it sure would have been nice to have met my brother. I have a lot of "brothers from other mothers" who are my fellow Infantrymen as well as every other man who has served our great nation. But it just isn't the same.

My brother was 39 when he died. A cousin later told me that he was sad that he wouldn't make it to his fortieth birthday. At one time my brother had been married and he lived with his wife near Portland, Oregon. When they divorced, he disappeared for a couple of years, living on the streets in Portland. While on the streets, he somehow contracted HIV. His death was due to complications with AIDS.

I have since met his ex-wife who is like a sister to me. I sought her out because I wanted to get a perspective on my brother from his former wife. I know that they loved each other and that my brother fucked things up with her. I could relate with that. It's a shame that we never got to be brothers.

## MOVING TO A NEW UNIVERSITY (2014)

In the late Fall of 2013, I decided that I wanted to pursue a master's degree again. But this time I wanted a degree in a field in which I had a working knowledge: business. I looked around for a reputable, regionally accredited university to earn a Master's of Business Administration (MBA). My choice was Grand Canyon University.

I began attending in February 2014 and enjoyed the classes. Later in the year, I realized that I was burned out at the Boy Scouts and that my son had two parents who both were working 60+ hours a week. My wife and I discussed our options, and we decided that I would become a stay-at-home dad and a full-time student. I left the Scouts three-and-a-half years to the day I was hired.

## GETTING MY MBA (2015)

After leaving the BSA I continued to work on my MBA. I was getting close to finishing up my courses and was invited to graduation in the Fall of 2015. We took the weekend and attended the graduation. My daughter, son-in-law, and our son went with us. It was good for my kids to see me graduate with a master's degree.

In December of that same year, I completed all coursework, and my degree was posted to my transcripts. I was especially proud of myself because I graduated with a 4.0 GPA. By this time, I had already decided to begin work on a doctorate the following year.

## GOING TO CULINARY SCHOOL (2015-2016)

Other than being present for my son and taking the lead in the other things my wife and I decided I would do, the beginning of my doctorate seemed to leave a gap in my life. I needed something to do that would get me out of the house because an online degree was isolating me even worse than usual.

My daughter was in culinary school at the time, getting ready to graduate. Everything she was doing in school sounded like fun, so I decided to attend culinary school as well. And let me tell you—I had a blast!

I never completed the degree because other things came up in life that required my attention: things I could not avoid. I hope to go back one day and finish. Just for the fun of it.

### TIPS FOR ADOPTEES
*Do Some Research to Better Understand Your DNA Results and the Search Process*

- *Facebook groups such as Search Squad have a variety of information. Read it and read other searchers' posts.*

- *The sites have a variety of information that will help you to better understand DNA and your results. Read it!*

- *Do other research on the Internet. You could use Wikipedia as a starting point if you'd like, but look for reputable sites that provide solid information and data. You want the best information available so that you can get the best results.*

## CHAPTER 12
# The Greatest Show on Earth
### All Hell Breaks Loose

*Don't let your thoughts run away with you,*
*don't start planning to bail out because you're worried*
*about the future and how much you can take. Don't look*
*ahead to the pain. Just get through the day.*

MARCUS LUTTRELL

### STARTING MY DOCTORATE (2016)

As I mentioned earlier, I decided to pursue a doctorate during the final months of my MBA. I chose the same school I was attending for my MBA because I was familiar with its routine and knew how it would work.

I carried on the work that I had done in my MBA by pursuing a Doctor of Business Administration (DBA). I would take courses in familiar subjects, but the focus would be more theoretical than practical even though there was practical work to be done in each class. That was especially true in courses such as accounting, economics, statistics, and quantitative methods.

## THE ANCESTRY.COM MESSAGE ("DO YOU KNOW WHO I AM?")

Sometime in 2014, I took a DNA test through Ancestry. While I told myself that I was specifically interested in discovering my ethnic background, I always had the hope that I would find a match to a close relative, identify my birth family, and hopefully find a sibling (preferably a brother). By this time in my life I had given up hope that I would ever find my parents.

Of all the scenarios that I had imagined over the previous 35 years since discovering that I was adopted, the one where I learned that my parents were dead was the one that always stuck in my mind. Every time I thought of this, I became overwhelmed with a profound sense of disappointment and frustration.

Of course, there were other scenarios I had considered. Most of them were depressing because most of them ended with the realization that I couldn't find my parents. Finding one parent while the other had already died was also one of the numerous scenarios.

The overarching theme when thinking of these scenarios was rejection. *Why did my parents reject me? And if I found them, would they reject me again?* All of this was very stressful and caused me anxiety.

I had also wondered for many years how finding my birth parents would affect my adoptive parents. In the end I decided that I would wait until they had passed before I started my search.

When I received my results, I did find out potential information about my ethnic makeup. But that part of the test wasn't as precise because it was based on sample populations that share certain DNA markers from countries and regions. Those results also change over the years as the sample grows and technology improves.

Also, each DNA testing service has different results. And while each might be similar, each is also different. But I was disappointed with the results when it came to DNA matches. There was a handful of "second cousins" listed and they were my closest matches. Unfortunately, I had no idea how to research to find my birth parents or potential siblings from that information.

Even now, while I am much better at researching matches, I don't think that I could figure out who my birth parents were from the matches I had then. I am good at locating people once I know who they are but not identifying people based on second cousins or more distant matches.

In the late Spring of 2018, I received a message from an Ancestry member. The member asked if I knew who they were. They also stated that we were related and asked if I knew the relation. I looked at the person's profile. It was evident to me that this person was my daughter even though her last name was not one that I recognized. But as the old saying says, "DNA never lies" and I stand by that.

While I couldn't believe it, I did not doubt that this person was my daughter. I looked at her name, trying to figure out who her mother was. That was key to verifying this information: if I didn't know who her mother was, I doubted that I was her father. However, as I said, DNA doesn't lie.

Looking at her profile, I quickly found out that she had a small family tree. I also discovered that a free account did not give me access to that tree. I did know that living individuals are not identified by name on an Ancestry public tree and that a tree someone grants you access to *does* show living individuals.

I figured that the cost of a monthly membership was worth the answer to her question. I paid, looked at her tree, and instantly recognized the surname of her maternal grandfather. The mystery was solved, and DNA didn't lie. I knew who her mother was and I recalled that I had a relationship with her in late 1989. She was the Belgian foreign affair.

I had already sent a message back to this young lady, stating that I had no idea who she was. But that was before I paid for the monthly membership and had my answer. Once I knew that the information was accurate, I needed to tell my wife first. I had been browsing the Internet in the bedroom while she was in our breakfast room doing schoolwork. Before heading out to talk to my wife I did a quick search on Facebook and found a picture of this person which I printed out. I joined my wife in the breakfast room and told her that we needed to have a discussion. I shared with her that someone had just contacted me through Ancestry and that I believed this person was my daughter. I then showed her the picture.

At this point, my wife and I had been married for almost 22 years, and the young lady looked like she could be 18. My wife asked me how old she was, but that was information I did not have. That was an awkward moment, and you could cut the air with a knife. I did mention to her that the young lady had to be older than 23, knowing that it was impossible that she was any younger. We decided to wait to see where that went.

I went back to our bedroom and crafted another response to my daughter's message. In it I said that I believed I had figured out what our relationship was. I also provided my telephone number and told her that I thought it best if she called. Talk about pins and needles! This was one time in my life when anxiety was eating me alive. I was hopeful that she would call or return the message that same evening. But I stayed up all night; there was no way that I could sleep.

By the time she called the next day, I was a bundle of nerves and literally was shaking. I almost could not answer the phone: I was shaking so badly that I was having trouble touching the screen in the right place. During that 24-hour wait period, I kept thinking about how I was so stressed that I actually might have a heart attack.

## THE CALL ("I WANT TO MEET YOU")

When she called, we talked for about an hour. I don't remember all the details of the conversation, but I do remember some. She had lived in Truckee, California for a while as well as Fernley, Nevada. She was living in Las Vegas at the time. When we spoke about college, she mentioned that she had lived in Santa Barbara, California, for a year, Knoxville, Tennessee for a year, and then Las Vegas. First, she attended community college and then the University of Nevada, Las Vegas. And would you believe it? She said that she had a bachelor's degree in Anthropology! What are the chances of that?

But the whole conversation was surreal. How would you feel, talking to someone who you learned was your 27-year-old child who had lived a lifetime before you even met? There was so much that I wanted to know and needed to know. There are some things that I still don't know, and I don't know if I will ever have those answers.

What will our futures bring? No one knows the answers to those questions. When ifs and unanswered questions are hard to handle, they leave a lot of uncertainty in a person's life. When that person already has a lot of uncertainty in his or her life, it just complicates things further.

One way to answer some of these questions was to have a face-to-face meeting. I asked her if she would mind if I came to Las Vegas to meet her. I do not believe that this was during this phone conversation. It might have been a follow up call that next morning.

She didn't have a problem with meeting me, and I asked her if coming down the next day would work for her. She said that would be fine. I told her that we would figure out the particulars once I was on my way.

## THE MEETING ("THIS IS MY DAUGHTER")

I headed out as early as I could the next morning and settled in for the seven-to-eight-hour drive. I didn't want to spend the whole day obsessing about the meeting, so I put on some music and turned up the volume. That didn't help anything. It was hard to focus on anything!

The drive seemed to take days. Each time I looked at the clock, it had barely moved. Each time I looked at the trip odometer, I had only driven a few miles. The last hour and a half or so were the longest.

I texted her when I crossed the Clark County line. I wanted to figure out where we were meeting. I knew that I would spend the night at my in-laws, and I knew that it might not be an optimal meeting place. If I were her, I would probably decline. But she said that meeting at their house would be fine. We set a time, and I figured that I would have about an hour to settle down before she arrived.

When I got to my in-laws, my brother-in-law let me in the house, asking why I had made the trip to Vegas. I shared with him that I was there to meet my daughter: not the one that he knew but one whom I had just discovered. He did a double-take and asked me to repeat what I had told him. So, I told him the story of how she had contacted me. He then asked me where I was meeting her, and I told him that she would be arriving at the house within the hour. I'm not sure how he felt about that, but the meeting took place. That was a good thing because there was no Plan B. He informed me that his parents would be coming home from a vacation in about two hours. That was something I hadn't been aware of, but it was what it was.

Before I knew it, the doorbell was ringing. My brother-in-law let me get it. There I was standing face to face with a person I had never met before: my daughter. We spent an awkward few seconds staring at each other before I said "Hey, come on in."

From there I can't tell you what happened. I know that I introduced her to my brother-in-law. He said that he was going to go upstairs to give us some privacy. We began chatting, and I knew that I only had about an hour before my parents-in-law would be returning home from their trip. I'm not one to keep a journal, so I must base what I know on what I remember. I will always remember meeting her, but what happened is fuzzy at best.

The next thing I knew, my parents-in-law were ringing the doorbell. I wasn't sure if it was them because I figured they would have the key to the door. But they had taken a shuttle home and didn't have their keys. My father-in-law asked what I was doing in Vegas, and

I asked him if they needed help with their luggage.

While I helped with the luggage, I went on to explain why I was in their home. I told them to not be shocked, but that there was a young lady in the living room to whom I would introduce them in a moment. I told them not to worry because after the introduction they would understand.

I walked with them to the living room and introduced them to my daughter. My father-in-law asked me what I had just said. I repeated myself.

"This is my daughter."

Both my parents-in-law just stood there for a few moments with their jaws on the floor.

My daughter was off work the next day, so we decided to go hiking at Red Rock Canyon. To lighten the mood, my daughter joked with me about being a killer who was going to throw her off a cliff. I joked back that how was I to know that she wasn't the killer? We both got a laugh out of the situation.

The hike was enjoyable. Later that evening when we said our goodbyes, I could not help but tell her that I loved her. That was a little awkward, but it is what it is. I knew that as time went by (if things went well), she would feel the same. But I told her that there was no pressure to feel the same.

Four years later while I'm sitting here in my in-law's dining room writing this, I am amused. It is currently December 27, 2022, and I started this memoir just a little over a year ago. So much has happened, and I am hoping to finish it while on this trip.

## THE CONFESSION ("I'M SORRY I LIED")

I did not tell my other kids that I was going to Las Vegas to meet the daughter I had never known: their half-sister. My son was just getting ready for finals in his junior year of high school, so we decided to not tell them until school was over.

When I returned home, I talked my wife into telling them even though there were still a couple of days before the semester ended. I also called my daughter and told her that she needed to come over because I had something to tell her and her brother. I had no idea how I would handle this situation, but I knew I would have to figure it out before the evening.

As has been usual for much of my life, I decided to cut straight to the point and go with the full truth. My daughter arrived and I got my son and her to have a seat in the den. Once they were seated, I told them that my cover story for going to Vegas had been just that: a cover story. I told them that I had gone to Vegas to meet a daughter whom I had not known about until just a few days before. They reacted similar to the way my in-laws reacted just a couple of days earlier. Their jaws hit the floor.

Once they started to recover, my son said that I had lied to them about going to Vegas, and he called me a manwhore for having three kids with three different women. Well, he was correct about the lie. I usually don't lie, but under some circumstances, I have found it to be necessary. Luckily, this was only one occasion, and I can't recall when the last time was that I lied to anyone.

It wouldn't be long after this reveal, that my son and daughter each meet their new sibling. Independently of each other, and then all of them together at my home. Unfortunately, it has been a long time since they have seen each other again, and I have no idea when or if that might happen. As of today, the three of them have only been together once. There isn't anything I can do about getting them together. They each are strong-willed and aren't going to do anything they don't want regardless of the reason. It would be great to be with them all at the same time, but I have no idea if that will ever happen again.

One thing that did occur through my daughters' meeting was that they convinced me to search for my birth family. They both thought that it would be a good idea, so I took their advice and tried to make that happen.

## SEARCH SQUAD

I knew from bumping around on Facebook that there were some groups dedicated to adoptees. I didn't have a clue what they were about or what they did if anything. I did figure that those groups would be a starting place to get my search moving. Whether or not they helped people or had information on how to go about a search, I assumed that whatever they offered would allow me to move forward on finding my birth

146

family.

I joined several groups looking to see what they might offer. One of those groups was Search Squad. I learned in this group they had connections to people who helped adoptees search for their long-lost families. I monitored the group for a short while, trying to figure out their protocol.

Once I had a clue of what the format was, I put my story out. Putting your story out is the way that you ask for help. You provide as many details as you can, and you hope that a searcher will help you.

## My Search Angel

The searchers that I mentioned are called Search Angels. Some people get a Search Angel quickly and others wait some time. The thing with Search Angels is that they all have their area of expertise. If your search falls into one of their areas, you will find an Angel. I don't know under what category mine fell, but I got a person who offered to be my Search Angel rather quickly.

The deal is that you must have had your DNA tested through one of the online services like Ancestry.com or 23andMe (the biggest two). If you haven't had your DNA tested, they will request that you do. This is how they make the connections: through your DNA. Some people get lucky, and a parent or sibling will pop up when they first test, or at some later time. The rest of us aren't that lucky.

The Search Angel requested access to my Ancestry. com DNA test. Now keep in mind that this is all happening either on Facebook or through Messenger. I told my Angel that I was uncomfortable with this, that I wanted to think about it, and that I wanted to do a little research about this on my own. She told me that it was completely safe and that she would only have access to my matches, their possible relationship, and the amount of shared DNA. I believed her, but I suppose that I was also a bit nervous. I took a couple of weeks to think this over before I decided.

## PERMISSION TO SEARCH

I finally reached back out to the Search Angel and told her that I was comfortable giving her access to my Ancestry.com results. When she replied, she told me that she had just had family come to visit and that they were planning to stay for a couple of weeks. She didn't have time then to work on my case, but she would reach out as soon as her family left.

I told her that was fine. After all, I was the one who hadn't allowed her to start on the search before and had waited this long. So what was another couple of weeks?

I waited until I heard back from her. Surprisingly, I didn't have any anxiety during that wait.

## THE SEARCH

It was about two weeks later when the Search Angle reached out to me and said that she was ready to begin the search. It just so happened that I had just taken a trip to Southern California with my daughter and was spending the weekend at my in-laws in Las Vegas. The Search Angel told me that she anticipated the search would take a week or so and that she would reach out when she was done. Now I started to get some anxiety.

A week or more seemed like forever, but I wasn't upset with the Search Angel. I knew that she would do what she could and that it took as long as it took. Maybe I was just nervous about what she would or would not find.

When we messaged it was about 9:00 p.m. I was able to get to sleep and get some rest which was a good thing.

## SEARCH CONCLUDED

At about 4:00 a.m. the next morning, I awoke to my phone dinging. A ding usually didn't wake me, and I had most of my notifications turned off during the night.

*Who the fuck would be trying to get ahold of me before the sun is up,* I said to myself.

I rolled over and looked at the phone. I couldn't read what the screen said because I did not have my glasses on. I found my glasses, put them on, and looked at the screen again. I immediately noticed that it was a message in Messenger and that it was from my Search Angel. I quickly wondered what was wrong or what information she needed that I hadn't already provided. I opened the message and it said that she had found my birth family.

I messaged her back and she responded that she had built a tree on Ancestry with most of the information that I needed. The tree included my mother, father, and four full siblings. I knew at that moment that this meant my parents were together for longer than just having me.

The Search Angel also told me that she had the unpleasant duty to inform me that my father and brother had already passed. That was truly unfortunate. We communicated some more, and then I had to decide what my next move was.

## THE LETTER ("I'M YOUR SON")

The Search Angel did not provide me with contact information. I told her that was fine. While it is hard to find someone who you don't know, it is easier to find someone with a name unless it is a common one.

But it didn't take me but a few minutes to find contact information for my mother and one of my sisters. The other two family members were more difficult to secure. But it didn't matter. If I could locate one of them, I believed that would be good enough.

I got an address and phone number for my mother

and one sister. I was too afraid to make a call, so a letter would be the way to go.

I wrote the letter over the weekend that I had been given the news by my Search Angel. As I mentioned, it just so happened that I was again in Las Vegas, staying with my in-laws. I had been there for a week or so but had traveled to Southern California with the daughter who found me a few months ago. We had gone to Disneyland and then down the coast to hit a beach for a day and for me to show her where I had lived in Southern California. I headed back home on Sunday and told myself that I would mail the letter the next day.

## The Call ("I'm Your Mother")

Just as I had planned, I mailed the letter on Monday morning and settled in for the wait. I had assumed that the letter would reach my mother in one to two days. Beyond that, I had no clue what she would do.

I had just returned home from picking up my wife from work the next day when my phone started to ring. I recognized the number as the number I had found for my mother. I went into the bathroom and answered the phone.

She was super excited to hear from me, and we talked for a few minutes. She confirmed that the information I put in the letter was accurate and that she believed she was my mother. I asked her what she wanted to do as a next step and she replied that we should meet.

I picked a Burger King that was close to her house, and she said that she would meet me later that afternoon. She would also have my youngest sister with her.

## THE MEETING ("WELL, I SUPPOSE THAT YOU ARE MY MOTHER")

Later that afternoon, I got ready and headed to Burger King. I was early because I wanted to get there before they did. Not only do I not like being late, but I also like being at a meeting first. I hadn't eaten for most of the day. When I got there, I ordered myself a Whopper meal with onion rings and sat in the middle of the restaurant, facing the door as I ate my meal. I had hoped that they would come in, identify me, and come right to the table. I figured that they had a good chance because I had described what I looked like and what I would be wearing.

That didn't happen. When they came in, I was sure who they were. They went to the counter and ordered, and then they took seats in an area where I could not see them. I quickly finished my meal and approached the two women, asking the older one if she was the name provided to me as my mother. She said yes and introduced my sister to me by name.

"Well, I suppose that you are my mother." She responded in the positive. We chatted for a while and then took a couple of pictures, agreeing that I would call my mother later and that we would work out meeting my other sibling who lived in the same area.

## FAMILY REUNION

After talking to my mother several times early in that week, it was decided that we all would meet at a local pizza place for lunch on Saturday and that my other local sister would attend as well.

By the end of the week, I found out that an aunt, a few cousins, and their kids would probably be attending as well. On the way to the pizza place that Saturday, I was sure that I was going to throw up. My wife and I got there and ordered. My mother and aunt showed up shortly after that. Soon after that, the cousins and kids showed up. My sister and her husband were late, something I later learned was a usual habit of theirs.

After eating pizza and talking to some of the family, we were all ready to leave. I invited my sister to go to the ice cream shop a few doors down. We had some ice cream and parted ways. I wasn't sure what would happen next, but I met more people that day who were relatives than I had ever imagined existed.

## THE TRIP ("SO, YOU ARE MY BROTHER?")

I planned a trip to Arizona within the next couple of months in order to meet my final sister. The drive down was much like the drive I made when I went to meet my daughter. When I arrived, my sister merely said, "So, you are my brother?"

It wasn't a statement. It was a question. I don't know if she really believed that I was her brother. I told her that our youngest sister had sent her DNA to Ancestry and that we would have confirmation soon. I knew that the test would confirm what most of us already knew, but that was me.

I was correct, by the way, and the test confirmed that my sister was in fact my sister. To this day, I still don't know if my oldest sister truly believes that I am her brother. That hurts me, but there isn't anything I can do about it.

## Loss #7 (The Pup Dies)

In January 2020 right as the COVID Pandemic was beginning, I got a frantic call from my daughter, the one that also lived in Northern Nevada. She told me that her beloved and beautiful Bulldog had just died. I was sad and asked her what the plan was. She said that her mom's ex-boyfriend had agreed to bury him on his property. Her husband, daughter, and she came and picked me up, and we made the hour-long trip out to the ex's house. He had already prepared the grave. My son-in-law put her pup into the grave. The ex and I covered it.

There is hardly a day that goes by that I don't think of that dog. He was beautiful, and I loved him very much. He was and always will be a part of my family.

## Tips for Adoptees
### Before Contacting a Potential Biological Relative, Please Consider the Following

- *Always reach out to a parent first. Try to find a parent. If you absolutely can't, then you could reach out to another relative. Contacting another relative could potentially ruin your chances if you find your parent later.*

- *Consider the other person's point of view. You have had time to prepare yourself, and they have not.*

- *As mentioned above, prepare yourself. Also, minimize your expectations. It is preferable to have no expectations. However, this can be extremely difficult.*

- *Choose a method of contact. The best methods are by telephone or a letter through snail mail (USPS). There might be other ways, but most say these two methods have the best results. A letter allows the individual to take time to decide how to respond. Remember, no matter the method of contact, you might never actually contact your relative or you might have a single contact with no possibility of any further contact. Make the very best of what you have.*

# CHAPTER 13
# The Ancestor's Tale

### RELATIONSHIPS

*Family is supposed to be our safe haven,
but very often it is the place where we find
the deepest heartaches.*

ANONYMOUS

## MY BIRTH MOTHER (BLOOD)

After meeting my mother and youngest sister in August 2018 and then additional members of family in the days and months afterward, I tried my best to form relationships with any of them who wanted to reciprocate my effort. I found it rather easy to have a relationship with my mother. Finding out that it wasn't her or my father who were at fault for giving me up made it easy to do. We began by talking every day. Soon, it progressed to me visiting her at her house almost every day. This continued for a while until another relative began spending time with me.

Nevertheless, I would call my mother each day, usually multiple times.

When I was spending more time with the other relative, I would still find a couple of times a week to visit my mother at her house which continued until COVID hit. That streak stopped for a period of 18 months because I was worried about having COVID and getting her sick. There were at least a couple of times when I didn't see her for six to eight weeks at a time. But the phone calls continued. During the remainder of the 18 months of COVID, we would try to have her over for dinner each week which we served in the garage. My niece would come with her many times.

In the late Summer of 2021 my wife and I took a 24-day trip, visiting friends, family, and some infantry brothers, driving almost 14,000 miles through 23 states. Once we were back, we began to have my mother over every Friday and Saturday night for dinner. On occasion, I still see her during the week. Maybe we meet for one of my niece's meets or go to lunch. I don't see this changing anytime soon. It seems to work, and I don't want to fix what isn't broken.

Of course, there are times when my mother irritates me. I guess that's natural. We have gotten into an argument or two and there has been a time or two when I haven't talked to her for a couple of days when we have been at a stalemate. We basically need to remember that neither of us are going to change. And if we want to continue our relationship, we just need to "deal with things" sometimes.

My pet peeve when it comes to my mother is that I hate it when she rolls over for other people. Maybe I feel strongly about that because I wouldn't expect her to do that for me. I tell her she just needs to stand up for herself, but she reminds me that she just isn't used to that. It's just too difficult.

While she can't really take my advice, she always seems to wish that my siblings would. She sees how I have more life experience than they do. That might be because I'm the oldest, have served in the military, have been a Reserve Deputy and Correctional Officer, and have more street smarts. We all have hard heads, and mine might be much harder than any of theirs. Sometimes, I dole out the advice and I keep it to myself at other times. It depends on many factors, especially with how exhausted I am with the situation.

## My Oldest Sister (Babysitter)

In some ways my oldest sister is the one with whom I have the most difficult relationship. When I first met her, I had the sense that she might not believe that I was her brother. Recently, we have communicated more than we have in a long time. She says that she loves me and calls me brother, but I sometimes feel that she's just not quite sure. It doesn't seem that she communicates much with our other siblings. Maybe their relationships aren't much different than ours.

While I don't give two fucks how other people feel or

think about me, my family aren't just people. They are family, and I do care what they think about me to the extent that we can try to have a relationship. I feel that she doesn't really know me, but then how could she?

I don't think that my sister knows what to talk about when we do talk, which could be because we don't know each other that well. It could be that she has made some assumptions about me, and maybe I've made some about her. The thing is that she won't just open up and tell me what she thinks we need to do in order to have a better relationship.

I have shared these thoughts with her in the past: I haven't held back. And though I have tried to stick to just telling her how I feel, I'm sure that I have told her what I think she *should* do. Obviously, I just call it like I see it. I don't have a filter with anyone. Welcome to the Infantry, bitches.

I would love to be closer to her, and part of the problem might be me. But if the problem is me, it isn't going to change. I live by a code, have standards, have expectations, and can't deal well with people who don't fall into line. I will just have to see how it progresses, but (like I mentioned) our relationship might not be that different from the relationship she has with our other siblings. The more I learn about siblings, the more I learn that some just don't get along. That's just life. I just don't understand that, but it's happening right in front of me.

159

## MY MIDDLE SISTER (BLONDIE)

Where to start? Holy crap. My middle sister is the relative who also wanted to spend time with me when I was spending time with our mother. When we started hanging out, she told me how jealous she was of the relationship that I had with our mother and youngest sister.

Frankly, I had my doubts if I would be able to have a relationship with this sister. It was just a feeling, but I'm sure she could come up with some reasons for my feeling this way. I feel she would be wrong. She was always saying that I was judging her, even when she wanted to hang out with me. She said she would never judge me and that I should give her the same respect. But I think she has that backwards. She would say my love was conditional, and I can assure you that it is not.

She broke the ice by inviting my wife and me over to her house for dinner. I already had a bad vibe about her husband, and I got the same vibe when we went over for dinner. I wasn't wrong. I couldn't see how she could be married to this man, but I didn't want to get into the middle of things.

We began spending increasingly more time together, hanging out, watching TV, running, and catching movies. Everything seemed to be going well, but it was clear that her husband didn't like me. I am sure he didn't because he knew that I knew what was going on within their marriage. The more time we spent together, the more I knew I was right about him. After some time, thank God, my sister decided that she was going to leave him.

I supported her throughout the whole process as best as I could. When the divorce was final (right at the beginning stages of the COVID pandemic), I could sense a change in our relationship. I didn't feel that I could spend as much time with her as I had before because COVID had me worried. However, I feel that this was a vital time when I should have been there for her.

We met up with our mother on her birthday in May and were going to take her to lunch. My sister told me she wanted to move away, and I was very upset at her decision. I ended up leaving and didn't go to lunch. That was almost three years ago. I haven't seen or talked to her except for a handful of times since then.

She has made choices that I and most of the family think are terrible. Granted, they are her choices. I do love her and don't want to see her get hurt. I feel such a connection to this sister that when she is hurting, I also hurt. In order not to hurt, I pretty much cut her from my life. I cannot take that pain.

## My Youngest Sister (Baby)

My youngest sister, her husband, and kids live with our mother. After initially meeting them, I got to spend a lot of time with them while visiting our mother. We are 17 years apart and she gets me going like

I'm the same age as her or like we are kids sometimes. When I started spending time with our middle sister, I spent way less time with her. She's a homebody, and it's hard for me to convince her to go out and do things. Another reason that she doesn't go out is because her family lives pretty much paycheck to paycheck.

Regardless, we communicate all the time. We text each other almost every day. Like all relationships, we have had a couple of disagreements. I feel that I am most like this sister than the others. After almost five years since finding my birth family, this is the sister with whom I have communicated the most. An interesting little fact is that she shares the same birthday as my wife. They celebrated their birthdays together a couple of times, but COVID and life has prevented that from happening every year.

## MY MATERNAL GRANDMOTHER (BITCH)

Not long after meeting my mother, she took me to meet her mom. I did my best to get along with this lady, but it was difficult knowing that it was her and her husband who forced my parents to give me up. She seemed nice enough at first, but I didn't get a good vibe from her. One reason for this is that she said they forced my parents to give me up *for my mother's benefit*. It would have been much better had she said that they forced my parents to give me up so that I would have a better life.

Shortly after meeting her, she told my mother that she

had some papers relating to my adoption. She would give them to us. Well, that never happened. That was cruel of her to do, and it fucking pissed me off.

When my middle sister was going through her divorce, she lived with this grandmother who bad mouthed me to my sister several times. This woman doesn't even know me and has the balls to badmouth me? Well, fuck her. I decided to have no relationship with her and just left her alone. Later, she told one of her sons (my uncle) that I had come to her house to threaten her. I have never been to her house unless I was with my mother or my sister. That is a flat out lie. Of course, my uncle believes her. What a gullible idiot.

The final straw came when my mother, niece, and I decided to go to a family reunion for my grandmother's side of the family. We went independently. Even though I knew my grandmother would be there, I wanted to meet my relatives and hoped they weren't like her. During the reunion she treated my mother like she was a little child. My 15-year-old niece noticed the same behavior.

We decided to leave the reunion right after lunch. My grandmother started berating my mother, and I had had enough. We exchanged words, and I told her that she was not going to treat my mother like a child. She told me that my mother was her daughter and she would do as she liked. I told her, "Not in front of me you won't." Then it *all* came out.

I addressed the elephant in the room: how she was

being a bitch. I even called her a bitch for good measure. Then I confronted her about how she had lied to her son, and called her a liar. She let me know that *no one* spoke to her that way and that she was in charge of the family. I told her that she wasn't anything special, and that, as far as I was concerned, she was a fucking, lying bitch.

After this back and forth (right in front of my mother) my grandmother said that she wished she had a shotgun to shove up my ass and blow my brains out. I told her to take her best shot. At this point we collected my niece who was upset that she had missed the fireworks, and we made our way into Yellowstone for the remainder of the day.

Since this incident, my mother has only talked to her mother once. She didn't want to, but her mother had called and insisted that she wanted to speak. My mother has seen just how horrible her mother was, is, and has been. She knew it when she was a young, pregnant girl of 15, but this really did it for her.

My wife and I consider ourselves to be intelligent, and we like figuring out mysteries. We use both our deductive and inductive reasoning when a mystery presents itself. The mystery that we have both been wanting to solve is the mystery of how my adoption played out. While the following is purely speculation, reasoning tells us that this is the most likely scenario.

*My adoptive parents couldn't have a child. They were upper middle class. We are sure that they put the word* out that they were looking to complete a private adoption. My dad did his business banking at a bank that was where our county courthouse now resides. He always worked with the vice president of the bank to take care of his business needs. When I was growing up, I met the vice president many times.

In comes my birth mother who provided me with some interesting information about her parents. Her father, my grandfather, was the vice president of the bank I mentioned. So, I had met my grandfather many times. The attorney that handled the private adoption had his office on the third or fourth floor of the bank, and he knew both my adoptive dad and my mother's father.

That reasoning brings us to the conclusion that my mother's father knew my adoptive father was looking to adopt a child. Ding, ding, ding! They struck a deal for me. I have no doubt that my adoptive father offered to pay for all the maternity care and the birth. I also have no doubt that he offered 20 to 25 thousand dollars to my grandparents.

My grandmother mentioned that they wanted their daughter, my mother, to attend university to study art. If my adoptive father knew this, he would have given that money to set this young woman up. And if he didn't, he would have given it to smooth over whatever troubles the situation caused. Again, this is speculation, but my adoptive father was generous, and he would do something like this because he would have felt that it was helpful. Even if the money was supposed to go to my mother, it did not. She never attended the university. She did, in fact, mar-

*ry my father, have four more children, and stay with him until death did them part.*

Another interesting point that I remember is meeting the owners of a local area sandwich shop when I was a child. In comes my mother again with information that the owners of that shop were her sister and brother-in-law, my aunt and uncle. My dad would frequent this shop often, picking up lunch for us and his construction crew. I distinctly remember my dad discussing with my mom the offer that the owners had made to him. They had offered him a franchise to open another location of their sub shop. My parent's discussion was quick, my dad had no interest because he had a thriving construction business.

So, that is some coincidence. I had also met my aunt and uncle when I was a kid, and they offered a franchise to my dad. I do not doubt that my dad didn't know that these people were my aunt and uncle, but he absolutely knew my maternal grandfather, the bank vice president was my grandfather. So, all these people knew each other and the circumstances of my adoption.

The final thing I speculate is that neither side ever wanted me to know, and each for their own reasons. My adoptive parents didn't want me to know because I was their only child, (My dad had a natural son with an ex-wife, but her new husband adopted the boy and my dad never had contact with them again. That certainly wasn't the man I knew. I wonder what the whole story is, but I fear I will never know), they loved me, and they were afraid of what I might do if I found my family.

My maternal grandparents didn't like my birth father, gave me away without his permission, forced my mother to sign away her rights, and also never wanted them or me to find the truth. It wouldn't surprise me if I found out that the money I believe my dad paid to them went to opening the first sub shop that my aunt and uncle owned. Wherever it went, it wouldn't have gone to where my dad intended it. My dad would have just been doing what he thought was right, and my maternal grandparent's greed got the best of them.

While my birth mother didn't speculate on the circumstances my wife and I laid this out to her one day. And do you know her opinion? *She believes that it is more likely than not that we are spot on.* I would like to see the papers that my maternal grandmother has, if she was even telling the truth. I would like to know if I am right or wrong. Barring the finding out of the actual truth, I believe that this is the most likely scenario. Ockham's razor suggests, "The simplest answer is usually the best one." This is the simplest answer.

Another interesting bit of information is that I attended high school with my aunt and uncle's daughters, my first cousins, and never even knew it. It is certainly a good thing that I never dated one of them! That would have certainly not been something to discover when finding my birth family! It is a wonder that someone didn't spill the beans at some point, but

I believe that everyone felt they had too much to lose if my parents found me or if I discovered them. Unfortunately, I have read that people like these (wanting to keep their secrets) are part of the reason that all adoptions in Nevada are Closed Adoptions.

The people who wouldn't have lost would have been my parents and siblings. How different would my life look now? In some ways, I would like to know. But in other ways, forget it.

## TIPS FOR ADOPTEES
### DECIDE WHAT YOU WANT TO SAY

- *Keep it simple.*

- *Provide minimal facts.*

- *Do not say, "You are my parent." State that you believe you are related and that you are curious to find out how.*

- *Allow them to deny or verify the relationship.*

- *Don't bombard them with questions. Let them take the lead.*

- *Don't force the conversation.*

- *Ask if you can give them your contact info. The ball is in their court at this point. If you go beyond, making further contact, you might ruin any chance you have to talk again much less ever meet them.*

## Chapter 14

# Darwin's Dangerous Idea

### What Lies Ahead

*Be Water, My Friend. Empty your mind.*
*Be formless, shapeless, like water.*
*You put water in a cup, it becomes the cup.*
*You put water in a bottle, it becomes the bottle.*
*You put water in a teapot, it becomes the teapot.*
*Now water can flow or it can crash.*
*Be water, my friend.*

BRUCE LEE

### Life Will Find a Way

I'm telling you: life is complicated. I assume that most people would agree with that statement. As I mentioned earlier, we each need to live our *own* lives and make our *own* decisions. Sometimes, that will put us at odds with others. However, that's a risk you need to take in order to have a purposeful life to some degree. Everyone wants to do what makes them happy, though that can hurt the ones we love. While some of us acknowledge that, there are others who want to be happy no matter the cost. I have found time and again that I pay a significant cost each time I try to make someone else happy in ways that can't be reciprocated. I try to make my family happy and hope that they will contribute to my happiness. That isn't always the case. I do my best, but I don't know how to handle these situations.

Twice, I have mentioned a friend of mine from my time of living in Southern California. When I visited Southern California last year, I tried to track him down. I located him pretty easily on Facebook and sent him a message in Messenger. It took a few days, but he responded and told me that he was living in the Sacramento area (a few hours away from where I live).

As we messaged back and forth, I learned that we had lived in the same town for a number of years. I distinctly remember my mother telling me that he was living in Tahoe at one point, but I had no idea he had been here in my hometown for almost a decade. I wish I had known that we were living so close together. Maybe we could have rekindled our friendship.

A few months after messaging him, we met in a Starbucks in Auburn, California, and caught up for a while. It was great to see him but sad that we had missed out on all that time. I hope we can stay in touch.

I also wanted to mention my first wife's biological father and my one-time girlfriend's biological mother. After I found my mother, my ex-wife asked me for some advice about her relationship with her biological father. It might sound like a cop out, but I told her that the best thing for her to do was what *she* thought best. I believe that she tried a couple of times to have a relationship with him, especially after her adoptive father (stepfather) died. I don't believe it worked out very well and I also believe he has since passed on.

My one-time girlfriend who had been in the Reserves found her birth mother and lived with her for a time. Before I found my birth family, I reached out to her to see if I could learn anything from her search. Unfortunately, I never heard back from her, though I did run into her once when I was hanging out with my middle sister.

## GRIEF & LOSS

As I wait for my car to be serviced this morning, I sit and wonder what life is about. Late yesterday evening, my daughter who lives here in Northern Nevada texted me to ask if I had seen that my aunt's husband had passed away. I had not seen or heard this information. This morning, I looked on Facebook and saw several posts about his passing. I was happy that she met someone to love after my uncle passed away. My uncle was my mom's brother, the one who had served in Korea and Vietnam, was a Los Angeles fireman, and would later work his own concrete business for many years. I thought back to when my wife, son, and I had attended my aunt's wedding to her new husband. He was a nice guy and I liked him. It was uncanny that he had the same first name as my uncle.

When I went to look for posts on his passing, the first thing that I saw was that a half-cousin of mine had passed away the day before. This really got to me. I hadn't even met this cousin. She is part of my birth family and is down the family line from my great-grandmother and her marriage to a man other than my great-grandfather (That is a little genealogy lesson for those that don't know about half relationships; you only share one of your ancestors and not a pair like full relationships. As the numbers increase, from the first cousin to the second cousin, the shared ancestry moves back one generation. In this case that moves from grandparents to great-grandparents).

The reason that this death got to me was that I hadn't had the chance to meet this cousin. She lived halfway across the country. I had been near where she lived in the Summer of 2021, but I didn't dare to reach out and visit. That's what it comes down to in many cases: the difficulty of reaching out to someone whom you don't know while simultaneously caring for them because they are family. Not everyone cares about their families, especially those that aren't close family members.

My immediate family was small growing up and there weren't a lot of extended family members with whom to interact because the family was spread out with only my parents living in Northern Nevada. What may not mean much to others means the world to me.

This story gets even sadder. From Facebook I had recently learned that my cousin's husband passed away about a month before her. It appeared that they hadn't been married for too long, just a few years. I knew that she had children from another relationship. So this family has lost in-laws, a stepparent, and other relatives all in a short period. I feel their loss, and I know it must be worse for many of them.

One of her brothers, another half-cousin, is the same age as me. I feel that I understand the loss of his sister. After all, I lost my brother. But is it the same? I did not experience my brother's loss firsthand. I didn't even know my birth family when he passed away. But the fact is that he was my brother, and he is gone. The rest of my family has had time to heal and for the loss to fade. But to me it is still fresh. The only way that I know him is through stories and photos.

All of this makes me think back to the loss of a first cousin once removed. Removed cousins belong to either the generations before or after your own generation. This person was my father's first cousin, so she was my first cousin once removed. I met her shortly after I found my birth family. She lived about 30 miles from me and had asked many other times for me to come to visit.

We all have the same problems and excuses sometimes. I didn't want to drive out there: not because it was a long trip but because it was time that I felt I didn't have. I made time for other family members, but why didn't I make time for her? Frankly, I'm not sure I know the reason. What I am sure about is that I *should* have made the time. She's gone now and there is no time to spend with her. That is an unforgivable loss.

Shortly after meeting my birth family, another half-second cousin reached out to me via a video call on Messenger. He used to live in Northern Nevada and had spent time with my mother and father in their youth.

Yes, just because someone is in the same generation as you, that doesn't mean that you are close in age. The best example I can give you of that is my youngest sister. She is 17 years younger than I am. This cousin was 17 years older than me. Between my sister and this cousin, both in the same family generation, there is a 34-year age gap.

Anyway, this cousin was nice and had reached out to me several times and I had hoped to meet him someday. That was another instance of something not to be. He passed away in January of last year. All I know is that he was in the hospital for a short while and had severe COVID-19.

I grieve for each of these people and their close families. Some are blood and others are not. They are in-laws or my adoptive family, but the losses are all the same to me. I wish everyone had that attitude. Life would be much simpler and better.

Grief is a strange bedfellow. We all experience it differently, just as we experience everything in life differently. We are all individuals which is what makes us diverse. But we also share many commonalities. There isn't a balance here and we will never truly know how others feel.

There is an old saying that says, "One of the hardest pills I had to swallow this year was realizing I meant nothing to people that meant the world to me." I am not saying that the people I just described are like that, but some of my closest family is and it is unfortunate. Why wouldn't someone want to be loved as I love them? I know they think that my love is conditional because of the way that I am. I am an acquired taste for many because I have a set of standards that I live by, but that doesn't mean that my love is conditional. It is not. I love these people more than they will ever know.

## THE COUSIN ACQUAINTANCE

Many years ago after my son began playing baseball at age 4, I met another baseball parent which isn't uncommon. I learned that her birthday was the same day as mine. Near the end of my son's career in Little League, I became the League's Player Agent. After I left the position, she took over and was the Player Agent.

Once I met my birth family while I was researching some matches on Ancestry and browsing Facebook, I noticed that my aunt was friends with this young lady's brother. I asked her about the brother, and she said that we were related. I even saw the brother in my matches on Ancestry. Later, this young lady took an Ancestry test, and she showed up as a match. I did some research and figured out the relationship. She is a half-second cousin on my father's side of the family.

So, it turns out that long before I met my birth family, I had already met someone *from* that family.

## OLD BATTLE BUDDIES

My relationship with my birth family is hit and miss, but I have also been doing some research to look for old Army buddies. These are people who served in the same unit that I did or just other Infantrymen who might have connections to the units with whom I served. I have connected with many people this way, especially within the last year.

Sometimes, I feel that these former and current soldiers are more of a family than my actual family. Admittedly, some of them tend to get on my nerves just like actual family members. But no matter what, any Infantryman is a brother of mine, and anyone who served is a brother or sister to me. I would do whatever I could for these men and women. But I also realize that while they all might say the same, some of them wouldn't follow through. That's just life.

I tried to find my old Executive Officer a couple of years ago. When I did find him, I learned that he had recently passed away from ALS. That was pretty heartbreaking to hear. He was a fine officer and was the one who gave me the news about my dad's final heart attack and helped me make arrangements to return to the mainland.

I had also been looking for my Army Recruiter for many years. True People Search and Facebook led me to some of his contact information. I reached out to him last year and he called me. I visited him in San Antonio, Texas, last Fall. It was wonderful to see him after almost 33 years. He hasn't changed a bit!

In the last chapter I mentioned a 24-day trip that I took with my wife in 2021. I also mentioned meeting some Infantry brothers. One of them was the Staff Sergeant (SSG) who was the Training NCO when I was the Company Clerk in Hawai'i. He is the first person from my unit with whom I reconnected. We had lunch at a BBQ joint in Bentonville, Arkansas, downed a couple of beers, talked about old times, and filled each other in on what we each had been doing in the last 33 years. This was truly amazing, and we stayed in touch. I tried to stop by and visit him last year, but his wife had just been in an accident and it wasn't possible. I am planning to see him later this year. I mentioned some of this earlier, but I wanted to touch on it again because we worked so closely together those many years ago and there is a lot of mutual respect between us.

I also got a chance last year to visit my First Sergeant and Company Commander from Hawai'i. I found each of them the same way that I had found my Recruiter. I visited my First Sergeant in Eastern Oregon after a trip to Boise, Idaho, for a Veterans' gathering.

He was happy to see me and remembered me well. I thanked him for all he had taught me. He was truly amazed that one of his men would seek him out and thank him. We are friends on Facebook now but haven't communicated much since. For me it would be easier if I had his number instead of just Messenger. However, I do hope to get up his way again soon since he's thinking about moving back East.

I spent the night a few months later at my Commanding Officer's house just south of Fort Benning. He was curious as to why I wanted to reconnect, but he was also appreciative. The visit went similarly to the way it went with my First Sergeant. I had enjoyed serving under him, he had taught me much, and I wanted to thank him. I also plan to see him again sometime in the not-too-far-off future.

Reconnecting with the people from my unit in Hawai'i has been one of the greatest experiences I've had in a long time. While they were all my superiors, they were all also my brothers because we all were Infantrymen. I wouldn't be who I am now without them. They are family and they help to alleviate some of my pain.

If only the Executive Officer were still alive, we would have the whole Scooby Gang. I believe we have all talked since I found them, save for the Commander and First Sergeant. Don't hold me to their not talking as being intentional, Don't hold me to their not talking as being intentional, if they haven't. That might be an oversight on my part, and I will try and remedy it if it is.

Now, all I have to do is figure out how I can get all four of us together. That would be the shit.

## ISOLATION

In the end I am just as isolated as I have ever been. People only have so much time that they can dedicate to others. I am no different, though I try to give as much time to my family as I can. Sometimes that is more time than I should.

It is important to me to connect with family (and that includes my military brothers and sisters). However, nothing fills the void like spending time with my children, siblings, and, yes, my mother. These are the people who should be the closest to me. It always sucks to find out that those you love the most don't love you in the same way. I know that doesn't mean they don't love you, but the inequity is something with which I have real trouble.

There is so much more to my story, but I am not ready to share some of those stories. I hope that what I have shared is useful to you in a way that can help give you insight or closure in your own journey to find your birth families. I don't want others involved to be brought into the spotlight because of me. It's a fine line, and I hope I have done my best only to highlight my aspirations, failures, successes, and my dream of family. I have intentionally been vague in many places, especially when it comes to names, but I hope that enough of my story comes through as I intended.

*Do You Know Who I Am?* has mainly been about adoption, trust, love, and understanding. In my life *everything* is about adoption, *everything* is about family, and *everything* is about the military. My life flows and sometimes crashes. I try to be what I need to be as situations arise. I am not always good at everything, but I try to "Be Water, My Friend," adapting as necessary. Peace out, all you Glorious Bastards!

## Tips for Adoptees
### Decide What You Want to Say

- *Keep it simple.*
- *Provide minimal facts.*
- *Do not say, "You are my parent." State that you believe you are related and that you are curious to find out how.*
- *Allow them to deny or verify the relationship.*
- *Don't bombard them with questions. Let them take the lead.*
- *Don't force the conversation.*
- *Ask if you can give them your contact info. The ball is in their court at this point. If you go beyond, making further contact, you might ruin any chance you have to talk again much less ever meet them.*

# EPILOGUE
## "Now You Know The Rest of the Story"

### THE FINAL FRONTIER ("AND THAT'S THE WAY IT IS")

A little over a month ago I began the search for an editor/publisher to help me polish this memoir and get it on the market. I didn't have a clue as to what I was doing. I reached out to a publisher that had published an adoption memoir that I had recently read sometime last year in anticipation of being at the point where I had completed my manuscript. I didn't feel that they were a good fit. When the manuscript was completed in December of last year, I reached out to another couple of publishers. They were even more of a bad fit.

Last month I read a memoir written by a Combat Infantryman that I really enjoyed. I said, "What the fuck, I'll reach out to his publisher," but I wasn't very hopeful. This turned out to be one of those situations where fate intervened. The publisher and I hit it off and he was intrigued by my story. How fortunate for me! We have been going back and forth on edits for the last couple of weeks and have had some phenomenal conversations. I can tell a story (Or so I believe), but I don't have creative vision. My publisher has that vision.

As I sit here writing this Epilogue and consider our initial meeting, I am thankful that he fell into my life. Even though I sought him out, the meeting was heaven-sent.

No matter how hard I work in life, I can't ever seem to create my own opportunities. I seem to roll along until opportunities present themselves, which is what I believe happened in this case. I always plan things out using the SMART Method to set my goals. SMART is an acronym for: (S)pecific, (M)easurable, (A)chievable, (R)elevant, and (T)ime-based. It is hard to achieve anything without goals. However, my opportunities always seem to be controlled by some higher power, no matter how strategic I am.

Before I end this last chapter, I want to share something. In cases of newborn adoptions at the time of my birth, the birth parents were strongly cautioned against naming their child. For parents giving up their children, there is no essential purpose in naming a child. For birth parents forced to give up their child, however, naming can create a bond—even if born out of desperation.

Such was the case with my birth parents, for I learned from each of my siblings that my birth parents told each of them about *me,* the child they had to give up. Not only did they know my story, but they also knew the name my powerless birth parents had given me which is also recorded on my original birth certificate: *Adam Bomb Day.* The message that my birth parents cleverly embedded in my name tells me all I need to know: *I was wanted.* I was wanted so badly that being separated from me had implications for them of atomic proportions.

This memoir has allowed me to relive some of the events in my life, many traumatic and some that are heartfelt and special times. There is still a lot of life in front of me (At least I hope there is), and I hope this memoir helps me to live it to my fullest. Maybe now I can trust, understand, and love those near to me better than I ever have, because I hopefully understand myself more for sharing with you, the reader. It has allowed me to tell a part of my story, of which there are many other parts. I hope to share some of those other parts in the future. But for now, all I have to say is, "And that's the way it was."

## TIPS FOR ADOPTEES
### DNA NEVER LIES!

- If *the match is labeled PARENT/CHILD, that person is your parent or child with one possible exception. Verify the amount of shared DNA measured in centimorgans (cMs). It should be between 2376 and 3720 cMs with an average of 3485 cMs. If the shared DNA is less than 2376 cMs (I've seen this twice) then there was an error in the labeling of the relationship. Always go by the shared DNA and not the predicted relationship. This does not mean that your test is invalid. It's just that the label of the relationship is incorrect. There are very few invalid tests. If DNA extraction does not go as planned, the company will ask for another sample. I can't recall another good example, but it would be pretty obvious that there is an error. In that case, you should reach out to the DNA company. None of this means that DNA lies. When testing is performed properly, the DNA, in fact, NEVER LIES.*

- *Learn how to use the chart at: https://dnapainter.com/ tools/sharedcmv4. This chart shows the range for a variety of relationships along with the average shared cM's. This is one of the most useful tools regarding DNA testing.*

- *Understand that the higher the shared cM's, the more reliable the match is. What that means is that if a match shares 3485 cM's, that match is only your parent or child. A shared match of 1740 cM's could be a number of possibilities including your grandparent, aunt or uncle, niece or nephew, half-sibling, or grandchild. The lower the shared cM's, the more potential relationships. Sometimes potential relationships can be eliminated due to a variety of circumstances. If you need help figuring it out, reach out to someone who can help such as the Facebook group Search Squad.*

# Acknowledgments

Being an adult is different than becoming a man. I left home at 19, still a boy. Over the next 13 weeks I became a man. I spent that time at Harmony Church, Fort Benning, Georgia. They say Harmony Church is 7 miles from Columbus and 2 feet from Hell. Three men ran Hell: Sergeant First Class (SFC) Lockwood, and Staff Sergeants (SSGs) Harris and Cruz. These Drill Sergeants and many like them turned Wayward Boys into men.

Sometimes, we need to be led. I had some great leaders when I was in the Army. Because those leaders are mentioned in my memoir but not named, I will identify them by their positions in Headquarters and Headquarters Company (HHC), 5th Battalion, 14th Infantry. They were my Company Commander (CO), First Sergeant (1SG), Executive Officer (XO), and the Training NCO. They all retired from the Army, and I thank them for their service. The Right of The Line!

We all need mentors whether or not we know it. I have been fortunate enough to have two mentors. Both taught me a lot about humanity. I met Dr. Julia Hammett the first day I started attending the local community college while trying to attain my second associate degree. Besides teaching me about Anthropology and humanity, she made me realize that I hadn't set my goals high enough. This memoir wouldn't exist without the guidance she gave me long ago.

The second was Dr. Thomas Vetica. Dr. Vetica was also a professor at the local community college in the Anthropology Department. He taught me that Anthropology could be applied to real world in areas such as business. Unfortunately, Dr. Vetica passed away while I was attending the University, and he is dearly missed. While I didn't quite follow the path that either of these professors envisioned, their guidance led me to a post-graduate degree and to the doctorate that I hope to finish soon: both in the field of business. Also, without them I would never have undertaken the writing of this memoir. They made me enjoy something that I did not like: writing.

Even though I sat my ass down and wrote this memoir, I had no clue how I was ever going to get it published. In came Robbie Grayson of Traitmarker Books. He worked his magic, took my story, and made it what you are reading. Truly, this book wouldn't be what it is without his creative genius. I couldn't ask for a better publisher, and I hold him in very high regard.

CHRIS HARVEY | RENO, NEVADA

# PHOTO GALLERY

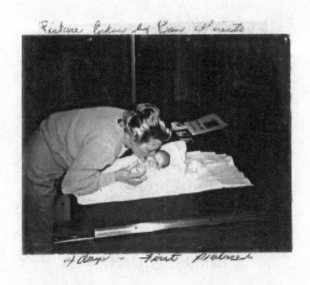

The first photo of me four days after my birth

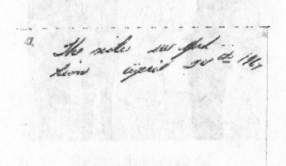

This is the inscription
on the back of my first photo

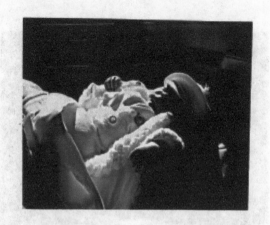

*Riding in the car with no car seat
right after my parents picked me up*

*My Baptism (left to right)
My dad holding me, my mom,
my Godparents by proxy, and my dad's mom*

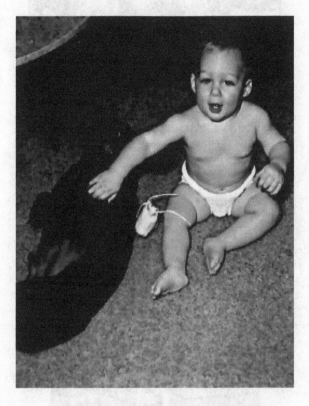

*Me and JimmyJohn. He's the dog
we tragically lost before moving to California.*

*My parents and me having dinner at the Mapes Hotel*

*Me in a school play as King Cole*

*With my Godmother's niece (or grandniece)*
*the summer we hung out on the farm*

*At a construction site with my dad*
*in the early 1970's*

This is in my Godparents' new home in Southern California (Christmas 1975). My dad is 5'10' and I'm just about as tall as he is at 8 years old. I was a big boy!

*Here is my childhood room, which is arranged
exactly as it was on the day that my mother told
me that I was adopted. I was sitting
in that chair and at that desk.*

My uncle in Vietnam

My uncle's medals from Vietnam and Korea, and my Infantry Cord which he would have earned as well.

My uncle's Combat and Special Skills Badges from top to bottom: Combat Infantryman Badge, Master Parachutist Badge, and Army Aviation Badge

*My aunt and uncle (the Combat Infantryman)*

Me Australian Rappelling off the Chopper Skid on the side of the Rappel Tower at Ft. Ord. This was our JROTC trip in 1985.

My last birthday with my dad before he died. The person on the far right is one of the two brothers with whom I was friends and whom I mention in my book.

*Dad and me in the Company Office the day before graduation from basic at Harmony Church, Ft. Benning, GA (August 20, 1986)*

*Me and my friend Ibo, Ferdinand Ibabao (right) on August 21, 1986, at Harmony Church, Ft. Benning, GA.*

*Me with the older of the two brothers with whom I was friends (left). He passed away recently. We both shared much respect for Bruce Lee.*

Pōkahuloa Training Area, Island of Hawai'i, HI.
Even though I drove in support of this
deployment, I also humped it just like all the
other Grunts. We had to keep up our skills.

Me in the field near Subic Bay, Philippines.
This was the deployment where I was awarded
an Army Achievement Medal.

*While not mentioned in my memoir, Colonel Alexander Lemberes was another one of my role models. He lived in Northern Nevada and was a friend of the family while I was growing up. He was the Commander of the 5th Special Forces Group in Vietnam for a short while. The picture carries a personalized inscription from him to me.*

*Me on the set of Tour of Duty
with Terence Knox, ("Zeke") on my left.
Schofield Barracks, circa 1987.*

*Top to bottom: My dogtag, my uncle's Parachutist Badge
from Jump School, and my uncle's dogtag
(Service numbers are whited out)*

**DEPARTMENT OF THE ARMY**
820TH UNITED STATES ARMY RESERVE SCHOOL
BUILDING 940, PARKS RESERVE FORCES TRAINING AREA
DUBLIN, CALIFORNIA 94568-5201

REPLY TO
ATTENTION OF:

01 JUNE 1991

MEMORANDUM TO SPC Harvey, Christopher E., Co C 820th Engineer
BN (C) (C) Reno, NV 89502

SUBJECT: Memorandum of Recognition

1. During the Period of January / June 1991 SPC Christopher
E. Harvey SSN: , while enrolled in the 54B Course,
(Nuclear, Biological and Chemical) Phase 1 displayed exemplary
academic achievement.

2. Out of the class of 15, you had an average of over 95 percent during the entire course. Your enthusiasm and ability to
interact with the Instructor and Students greatly contributed
to the success of the class.

3. The example you set during the course, reflects on you,
your command and the United States Army.

4. Request a copy of this letter will be placed in your Official Military Personnel File.

ROGER A. EDWARDS
MSG, E-8, USARF
Course Director 54B

cf: Co,C. 820th Engn BN (C) (C)
Reno, NV 89502

*Letter recognizing outstanding performance at 54B School
where I taught approximately 1/3 of the courses*

*This NBC calculator was a tool of the
trade, in the 80's and 90's for a
Chemical Operations Specialist
(54B). NBC stands for nuclear,
biological, and chemical.*

# DEPARTMENT OF THE ARMY

## SPC CHRISTOPHER E. HARVEY

## IS OFFICIALLY COMMENDED

### FOR

HONOR GRADUATE

CRITICAL OPERATIONS SPECIALIST COURSE (54XX)

17 JUNE 1991 - 28 JUNE 1991

SIXTH ARMY SCHOOL, DUBLIN, CA 94568-5201

_____          _____
        28 JUNE 1991                    JESSE C. PARRISH
                                    LTC, QM, USAR
                                    DEPUTY COMMANDANT

*Honor Graduate Award*

# DEPARTMENT OF THE ARMY

THIS IS TO CERTIFY THAT THE SECRETARY OF THE ARMY HAS AWARDED

## THE ARMY ACHIEVEMENT MEDAL

TO    PRIVATE FIRST CLASS CHRISTOPHER E. HARVEY

FOR    exceptionally meritorious achievement during exercise "Balikatan 87" from 28 November to 21 December 1987 while assigned to the Support Platoon of the 5th Battalion, 14th Infantry. As a HEMTT driver tasked to logistically support the line companies, PFC Harvey handled with distinction a grueling driving schedule over difficult terrain in order to provide chow and ammunition on a timely basis. PFC Harvey's efforts were instrumental in the logistical success of the exercise. PFC Harvey's outstanding performance of duty reflects great credit upon himself, his unit, and the United States Army.

GIVEN UNDER MY HAND IN THE CITY OF WASHINGTON
THIS 16th    DAY OF    January    19 88

_____                              _____
Ron E. Wadding, LTC, IN                                  John O. Marsh, Jr.
Commanding                                               SECRETARY OF THE ARMY

*Army Achievement Medal*

## Be it known that

PFC HARVEY, CHRISTOPHER B.

has successfully completed the
Individual Infantry Training
At The United States Army Infantry Center
and that in testimony
thereof is awarded this

## Diploma

Given at Fort Benning, Georgia, on this the
21st day of     AUGUST     nineteen hundred and eighty- six

R. S. Siegfried

Colonel of Infantry
Commanding

FB Form (ITB) 81  9 Mar 76

Certificate for OSUT (One Station Unit Training)

The United States of America

honors the memory of

**EMMET J. HARVEY**

This certificate is awarded by a grateful nation in recognition of devoted and selfless consecration to the service of our country in the Armed Forces of the United States.

Ronald Reagan
*President of the United States*

My Dad's Service Certificate

Professional Development-Level 1
#1105

BOY SCOUTS OF AMERICA
CENTER FOR PROFESSIONAL DEVELOPMENT

*Group picture from Professional Development Level 1.*
*Basic Training for Professionals of the Boy Scouts of America.*

The Boy Scouts of America Through the
**National Council Staff at the Center for Professional Development**
Awards This Certificate to

## Chris Harvey

In Recognition of the Completion of

### Professional Development Level 3

In witness whereof the seal of the Boy Scouts of America is given
this 7th day of February, 2014

BOY SCOUTS OF AMERICA

*Certificate from when I attended Professional Development -*
*Level 3 which was the end of the initial training*
*for Boy Scout Professionals*

*My birth parents*

*My brother*

*My three kids. Left to right: my oldest who located me through Ancestry.com, my "Firstborn," and my youngest.*

*Me and my 3 surviving siblings
along with our mother (my birth mother).
From left to right: my youngest sister, me, my middle sister,
our mom, and my oldest sister (in front of our mom).*

*This was my daughter's beautiful English Bulldog*

## About the Author

CHRISTOPHER E. HARVEY was born and raised in Reno, Nevada, but also spent two impressionable years as a child, growing up in Escondido, California. After high school, he joined the United States Army as an Infantryman, serving with the 25th Infantry Division (Light) in Schofield Barracks, Hawaii, from 1986 to 1988. He returned home when his dad passed away and joined the United States Army Reserve serving as a chemical operations specialist in the 124th Army Reserve Command in Reno, Nevada, from 1989 to 1992. He received a Bachelor of Arts in Anthropology from the University of Nevada, Reno in 2008, and a Master of Business Administration from Grand Canyon University in 2015. He worked in the retail grocery industry for almost 20 years before working as an executive for the Boy Scouts of America from the early- to mid-2010s. He is currently working on his dissertation on Service Failures in Retail Grocery for his Doctor of Business Administration. He is active in Rotary and several Veterans Service Organizations. Chris currently resides in Reno, Nevada, with his wife Katherine. He has three grown children.

TO CONTACT THE AUTHOR...
*facebook.com/11HotelGrunt*

"An important addition to boots-on-the-ground historical accounts of Sadr City, Iraq..."

**BOONE CUTLER** | Author of Callsign Voodoo

# NO SHIT HERE I AM

### A SOLDIER'S STORIES OF LIFE DURING AND AFTER THE WAR ON TERROR

## JARROD L. TAYLOR

*Available on Amazon*

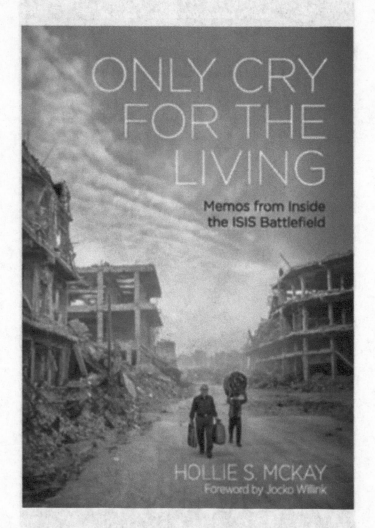

ONLY CRY
FOR THE
LIVING

Memos from Inside
the ISIS Battlefield

HOLLIE S. MCKAY

Foreword by Jocko Willink

*Available on Amazon.com*

13th Anniversary of The Surge
COMMEMMORATIVE EDITION

# ANGELS
## in
# SADR CITY

*We Remember...*

With Memoirs & Tributes by
**#sadrcityboys**

*Available on Amazon.com*

# The Spartan Pledge

## >TAKE THE PLEDGE TODAY<

"I will not take my own life by my own hand
without talking to my battle buddy first.
My mission is to find a mission
to help my warfighter family."

**facebook.com/TheSpartanPledge/**

9 781088 120156